Those Were the Good Ol' Days—Or Were They?

Those Were the Good Ol' Days—Or Were They?

Hilarious Stories
of Days Gone By

Bud Cunningham

VANTAGE PRESS
New York

Text and cover illustrations by Kasi Davis

FIRST EDITION

Published by Vantage Press, Inc.
419 Park Ave. South, New York, NY 10016

Manufactured in the United States of America
ISBN: 0-533-15423-5

Library of Congress Catalog Card No.: 2005910840

0 9 8 7 6 5 4 3 2 1

To my wife, Liz, for her help in producing this book; my dad and mom; my sons, Josh and Shane; and the folks of Tillamook for their support. To the folks of Nova Scotia, for all the wonderful memories. Special thanks to my sister Ethel for all her help.

Contents

Acknowledgment   ix

  1. Old Smokey   1
  2. Now That's Fast   12
  3. Three, Two, One, Blast-Off?   23
  4. Hurricane Hazel Strikes Again   34
  5. Hurricane Hazel Versus Whip Lash Jake   46
  6. A Real Catchy Tune   57
  7. What's Your Nick Name?   69
  8. Willie's Secret Weapon   78
  9. River Man Tom Pickering   90
10. Cloud Nine   100
11. The Corn Family   110
12. Like Father, Like Sons   122
13. Talk about Cheap!   132
14. The Neahkanie Treasure   142
15. They Got the Ax   151

Acknowledgment

Special thanks to Kasi Davis for her professional illustrations.

Those Were the Good Ol' Days—Or Were They?

1

Old Smokey

If anyone reading this story ever had an outhouse in the good old days, you won't have any trouble relating to this story. Back in Canada, the year 1951, we had a three seater, two for the adults and a low one for us kids. It was the custom to cut a half moon in the door, more for ventilation than anything else. At the time it was supplied with Sears catalogs and yellowish dried newspapers which served several purposes, one was reading; the other I won't mention.

During this time in history my dad smoked cigarettes, and to avoid Mother's complaining he used the outhouse to puff his smoke and to catch up on his reading. He had a tin can setting there to doff his finished cigarette butts, so this one day cousin Harry and I had to do some business in there when we noticed a few only half used. I was six years old and Harry was seven, also full of wisdom or so I thought. We decided to fire them up even though Father always warned against it with his finger shaking, saying, "Tobacco is a weed, the devil planted the seed, it ruins your clothes, soils your hands and makes a dirty smoke stack out of your nose." I thought about this, and told Harry I changed my mind, but he called me a wimp as he struck a wooden match across the wooden boards. I watched him torch the non-filter thing as he stuck the flaming match in front of my face. Even though I knew better, I partook of his invitation as the taste of tobacco tarnished my lungs for the first time. Coughing now took control but somehow we managed two puffs each, then Harry said watch this—as he drew a huge puff trying to exhaust it through his nose. He suddenly went into a coughing spell and started crying. I laughed and called him a wimp but when I looked at him my laughter turned to horror. He always had a crew cut, and now his face was a light shade of green. He looked like Frankenstein.

My screams scared the birds away that were nesting in the roof. We threw down our lit smokes and ran to the rhubarb patch as we threw up all over everything. After laying there for a half an hour, I heard sister Ethel yell, "The outhouse is on fire."

We sat up as flames streamed from the back—we were terrified as Dad grabbed buckets and raced to the well. Everyone was yelling, as my uncles formed a bucket brigade. Harry and I joined the line still weak and sick, as bucket after bucket was splashed on the hot fire. Finally the flames disappeared as steam and smoke still made ghostly images in the air. Father pondered over the partially burned outhouse and quietly comforted Mother by stating that it only burnt the back end and with some help it could be fixed. Big mouth Linda said she seen Harry and I run from there last. Father looked at us with cold eyes, they were glassy and wide and looked like a hoot owl in a herd of mice. He just pointed at the smoking outhouse without saying nothing, glared at us again as we burst out crying taking small steps backward. Well sir, the rest is history—and the only smoking we did after that came from our backsides.

Harry and I had to help Dad and Uncle Ed rebuild the outhouse. I was whacked several times with boards; Dad always said it was an accident, but towards evening Mother caught him getting ready to beam me a good one. She yelled and they really got into it. Mom made it hot for Father that

2

day as the heated discussion took place in the healing out-house. The last letter I got from Harry he stated that the old outhouse was abandoned but still standing along with the droopy old sign, mutely boasting its name, "Old Smokey."

Look at the Flashing Lights

We went down to see the lights like everyone else. It was hard to find a parking place, cars everywhere loaded with their families from the farms and town. The year was 1951, and the Canadian National Railroad was installing flashing lights and bells at the junction just before you entered town. What made the cheese more binding was the fact being that Uncle Bob and Uncle Nic and my dad were hired to work doing nothing complicated; they just dug holes and mixed cement. All the high tech wiring was done by the college guys from Halifax. The freight train was supposed to enter Shelburne at 6:30 P.M. We got there at 5 P.M. along with Dad and Mom, six sisters and little brother Dale.

Excitement ran high, I remember looking at the brand-new warning lights and just couldn't wait for the train to see them work. The mayor showed up with the town band. They mounted their instruments and started practicing the song "Casey Jones." Mr. Bower came ripping towards us in his old Model T, doing close to sixty miles per hour according to Aunt Hazel, and slid sideways in the road as parents gathered their kids to safety. He was completely out of breath when he jumped out and took several deep gulps of air while resting his hands on his knees. He was still wrapped with excitement, remarking to the eagerly listening crowd that he had just left Welchtown and the old store keeper told him the train was ten minutes ahead of schedule.

The crowd roared as goose bumps ran up and down my spine. The mayor ordered Dad, Uncle Nic and Uncle Bob to stand beside the new lights as he told the admiring folks that the threesome was mostly responsible for this history-breaking event. He demanded a huge applause; Mother started crying as the three joined hands with cameras flashing. It was now 6:15 as a few people stood on top of their cars looking up the tracks for black coal smoke, but no sign of the train yet.

Aunt Hazel made the remark that she had a touch of psychic power, which told her the train went off the track. She stated that such a machine should have never been built, too much power and weight, the earth just couldn't handle it. However, Louie put his ear to the track and yelled "She's coming." Soon we heard the whistle and black smoke could be seen. Aunt Hazel said she was just joking, but with all the loud excitement from the crowd, she was not heard.

The band now piped up and boy was I excited. Steam shot right from the boiler as the hissing and puffing reminded me of a dragon. Now every eye was fixed on the lights. The train was only fifty feet away and now it was crossing the road but no lights. We were surrounded by smoke and curling steam but no lights. Everyone blew their car horns, but no lights. The train and six box cars had passed, but no lights. Aunt Hazel said it was Dad and my uncles' fault. She said none of the three had ever done anything right in their life and this wasn't any different. The mayor made the remark that they may have cut the wires with their shovels or something.

Dad got mad and called Aunt Hazel a busy body and a big mouth. He told the mayor the only reason he got elected was because no one else ran for the position. Aunt Leafy threw Kool-Aid in Aunt Hazel's face. Dad pushed the mayor around and at the same time told him things he didn't like.

Friends and neighbors were at each other's throats. I was amazed to see such childishness, especially when the mayor stuck out his tongue at my dad and said "Na-na-na-na-na." Mr. Bradford pulled Charlie Snell's thick glasses off; Mr. Snell tried to push over a huge fence post, thinking it was Mr. Bradford. I couldn't help laughing. Things were getting out of hand so the police were called.

Six Mounties in three police cars with flashing lights arrived. Aunt Hazel told the Mounties that she tried to break up this situation but was punched in the nose as she pointed to the blood on her shirt. They could plainly see that it was strawberry Kool-Aid. After an hour everyone cooled down and shook hands. A lot of back slapping and apologies filled the air. One by one the cars pulled out and headed home. I was a little disappointed. We came to see flashing lights and we did, even though they weren't the ones we expected.

Mag Is Back

Gordon was a man who loved to scare us kids back in the '60s, every chance he got. He had a good outlook on life, just like Mother said, but his big mouth always got him into trouble. He met his wife Mag in a roundabout way. Father said Gordon was shopping one day for groceries and he approached the counter to check out his canned soup but had to wait because in front of him was a big woman who would slowly place one item at a time upside down on the counter.

Gordon was irritated by this so he tapped the lady on the shoulder and said, "You're single aren't you?"

Mag smiled and replied, "Oh you devil! You can tell that just by the way I put my stuff on the counter, can't you?"

Gordon sarcastically growled back, "Heck no, you're ugly."

5

Mag was six foot six with broad shoulders. She picked up Gordon and body slammed him—taking him down along with the entire pickle aisle. Gordon screamed for mercy as Mag started rolling up her sleeves, with one arm she picked him up by the hair and the slap sounded like a rifle shot as Gordon staggered toward the door. Seeing this a husky clerk grabbed her from behind—but later the ambulance driver told him, "I bet you won't do that again!"

Some say it was a haymaker, others said it was a right cross, but whatever it was, it made both Gordon and the clerk overnight guests at the local hospital. Somehow Mag and Gordon married. She had a thirteen-year-old son named Charlie, and most of the time the threesome got along quite well. For their honeymoon they decided to visit Portland, Oregon. They had never visited a city before so the excitement ran high when they boarded the plane in Idaho bound for Portland.

In minutes they were in the air, but Gordon's big mouth would soon ruin their trip. Gordon, Mag and Charlie sat in the rear of the plane. Gordon thought he recognized a friend near the front, an old logger named Jack. Gordon stood up, cupped his hands over his mouth and yelled, "HI JACK!" Passengers threw their hands in the air as screams reeked throughout the cabin. Some tossed their wallets and watches toward him in panic as the stewardess smashed a Heinz ketchup bottle over his noggin, which made the situation look gruesome. Mag stepped in and broke up the tussle—and after much discussion the problem was solved.

Finally they touched down in Portland and they were totally fascinated by the boxes as Gordon called them, actually they were elevators. Gordon stood in front of them for an hour. He seen ugly women get in them—the door would shut and seconds later a lovely lady would appear. Now to Gordon, this was magic. He took Charlie aside and told him to put his mother in that there box. I remember that Father said that Mag had more chins than a Chinese phone book, and her face would stop a train. Anyhow, Mag got in the box, the door shut and sure enough out popped a lovely lady when the door opened. Gordon was tickled pink as he gave her a tremendous hug—but to his dismay the lady screamed and ran away. He stood there confused, scratching his head when he felt his body raise. When he was slammed hard to the floor, just before passing out he murmured, "MAG'S BACK. . . ."

Hurricane Hazel

Everyone was excited all over town. The year was 1952, and everyone had only one thing on their mind, the big event. This made headlines all over the Maritime Provinces, which included Nova Scotia, New Brunswick, and Prince Edward Island.

Big Mack, the human bulldozer, was coming to town to challenge my Aunt Hazel in a boxing match. Big Mack's promoters had read about my Aunt Hazel in the newspapers. They were aware of her huge twenty-six-inch biceps and her four-foot-three-inch shoulders. She wore size seventeen shoes, her fist matched her shoe size. They heard how she could throw her late husband Uncle Ed a distance of forty feet if he didn't resist. Her upper leg muscles were thirty-eight inches around and she stood a towering seven foot six.

I was only seven years old at the time, but my pal Harry and I got to help build the ring and string balloons all around. The posters showed a picture of Big Mack, he was from Sweden—big nose and a massive body weight of three hundred pounds, compared to my Aunt Hazel he needed to gain fifty pounds to match her weight.

We loved our Aunt Hazel. She was our barber, doctor and now our hero. Two days before the match, a big white car pulled into town. The band, which my dad nicknamed, "What a Pity," tried to play "She will be coming around the mountain when she comes." No one knew the name of the tune until the mayor confessed to the folks the true title.

I remember how excited cousin Harry and I were when the Bulldozer stepped out of the car. He had a mad look on his face, but I couldn't help going up to him for an autograph. He ripped the pencil from my shaking hand, chewed it up, then spit the yellow wood in my face. It made my dad mad, he yelled at him but when Big Mack made the motion to come to him Dad hurried off, stating he heard Mother calling. Actually, Mother was right there holding my hand at the time. Then in a thundering voice he called, "Where is this freak you hicks call Aunt Hazel?" Then his rough laugh made cold chills ripple down our backs. As he walked off, I thought to myself, how in the world could anyone in their right mind step in the ring with such a moose.

Harry and I raced to Aunt Hazel's place; she didn't seem nervous as we repeated the news about the arrival of Big Mack, she just kept exercising with a hundred-pound weight, twirling it like a baton. Once done with that, she went outside to her wrecked Volkswagen, picked it up, gave it a toss, then kept rolling it over and over time after time, like a cat playing with a mouse.

Saturday morning rolled around, the ring was set up in our pasture. Harry and I helped unload the chairs that just arrived, over five hundred we counted. Then they nailed a big sign up which read, "Canada's Finest—Mack the Bulldozer versus Hurricane Hazel."

By three o'clock every seat was taken, as many more folks stood around ringside. We seen license plates from Quebec, Maine, and even Massachusetts. The announcer was a city slicker we didn't know, but when he announced Big Mack, most folks booed but hushed when the Bulldozer glared at them. When he announced my Aunt Hazel, Harry and I had to plug our ears, because the applause and clapping were deafening. Aunt Hazel had coveralls on that were way too small, so she left the sides unbuttoned. My dad whispered to Mom that it looked as though someone tried to stuff fifty pounds of mud in a twenty-five-pound bag. Mother pushed his face away in disgust.

Her homemade boxing gloves looked like two football helmets as her hair curlers waved as she jumped up and down. The bell sounded as the referee told them to shake hands. Aunt Hazel pulled off her right glove to oblige, Big Mack seen his chance and clobbered her with an awful smack between her eyes. Aunt Hazel barely moved. Later Dad said such a blow would have killed an ox. The Bulldozer was amazed as his eyes grew wide. Aunt Hazel pulled her glove back on, lumbered over towards the Bulldozer. Some said it was a right cross, others said it was a bear trap left, but whatever it was, Big Mack didn't know till the next morning as the doctor fused his broken jaw. The crowd cheered and the celebration went on well into the night.

Aunt Hazel once again was our hero. That same year we had a hurricane that smashed fishing boats and tossed cars around like toys. The weather bureau named the storm, yeah, you guessed it, Hurricane Hazel.

My Dad Walked on Water

Back in July of 1956 we lived on a small farm some six miles from town. Mom and Dad got together and produced eight kids. We had a big lake almost in our backyard where I spent most of my time. Dad and my uncles this one day decided to put a barbwire fence up smack dab across the middle of the lake. Dad said the purpose of this was to keep our cattle on our property in the summertime when the lake would get real low.

The fence posts were sank deep in the muddy bottom and placed only three feet apart. This one July day the lake rose about six inches above the posts after several days of heavy rain, which was very unusual. It just so happens a busload of tourists stopped to the west side and took pictures of the dark blue gleaming lake. Father was a joker, so seeing them gather there decided to make their day. He raced to the house and had Mother wrap him up in a white sheet, not telling him the reason as she started firing out questions right then left.

He walked to the lake, made sure they were watching, then started walking on the fence posts—not visible to the tourists. What a sight! The wind was blowing the white sheet as it flapped vigorously. When he was about halfway across he noticed them drop to their knees and start shouting repentance. One older lady passed out as the bus driver ran to her side. Others waded out knee-deep, demanding to be baptized. Seeing this, Father stopped for a minute and raised his hands high as the baggy white sheet flapped even more. The bus driver had his hands full baptizing, throwing liquor bottles away, and joining the tourists in singing hymns. Father made it across then disappeared in the thick bushes.

The news spread fast and after about five or six hours more buses appeared, now the shoreline was packed. Hymns rang out loud and clear—then a ruckus broke out, as the late comers didn't believe the pioneers. Father was still hiding in the bushes but now the hour was getting late, so now he made ready for his going home appearance.

He noticed another tour bus had arrived with band equipment. He waited until they were set up, then started his fence post walk back to the other side. A great noise sounded again as many more fell to their knees. Then an old man in a wheelchair somehow stood up! The band played "We shall gather at the river," as more cars and buses crowded at the small shore. Father guessed that there were probably three hundred people in all. He was so excited he started showing off, he twirled around in circles on the narrow post, then it happened . . . he became dizzy and lost his balance. The onlookers couldn't believe their eyes as he splashed headfirst into the cold water.

Father couldn't swim, so he screamed for help. Cousin Harry and I ran to the row boat and paddled out to the miracle man. Panic took him over as we groped for his air-filled white soaked sheet. We pulled him on board and finally headed for home. Now his believers turned on him as sticks and stones sailed all around us. Finally we got Father to the house, the band packed up and the buses pulled out. That following Sunday at church the preacher really embarrassed Father when he said, "All you who were at the river last week probably seen brother Grant fall in the water," and looking at Father said, "Oh thee of little faith . . ."

2

Now That's Fast

When we were kids going to school, the whole world was only five square miles, or so it seemed. We lived on a small farm back in Canada in 1954. I remember this one day we were to have a contest and the winner would claim a new bicycle. Each student under the age of fourteen was eligible to take part. There were forty-four kids who would participate, myself one of them. The contest rules were as follows: (1.) Subject was to be all about our dads. (2.) True, to the best of our knowledge. (3.) Something positive and good about how our dads had done something sometime really fast over the years.

When school was out everyone went their various ways. I was seated on the handle bars of my friend Harry's bicycle. I complained every time he hit a bump on that old gravel road leading home.

I rushed in the house, Mother was baking bread in the oven or the old Excel wood stove. I noticed she had one loaf in the warming oven above the stove, then she dipped hot water from the side tank. I told her all about the contest that would take place next month, and a new bicycle would be offered as the prize for first place. I asked her what was the fastest thing Father had ever done that she remembered. I could tell she couldn't think of nothing, so it was up to me.

Time sped by and by May 15th at 7 P.M. the auditorium at our school was packed with parents and folks from everywhere. Mr. Barkhouse, our principal, came out on the stage, but when he grabbed the microphone he got a terrible electric shock, it knocked him right backstage where he started from. Now the old maintenance man rushed out, wrapped the thing with black tape, making the claim that it was safe, even though he refused to touch it himself. The principal once again came out with both hands wrapped in linen, he then explained the rules to the contest, as many nervous dads listened closely.

Willy came out first. He bragged how fast his father could run, stating that he once beat the train to town on a ten-mile downhill race. Harry was next. He said that his father was two hundred and sixty pounds, almost seven feet tall, claiming that the fastest thing he ever did was grow. When my turn came I told about the time Dad was chased by a big black bear. He was running so fast all anyone could see was the bottom of his shoes, it looked as though he was lying down. That got me a good laugh. Tony stepped up next and spoke about how his dad threw a bill collector through the wall of their house so fast that that he closed the gap up behind him.

Phillip was next, he was from Halifax originally, but he and his family moved to our small town about two years ago. His dad had always been involved in politics and was well to do, as my Aunt Hazel put it. However, now he decided to get out of politics and he took a job working for the county. I often heard Dad say that Phillip's father never put in a full day's work in his life; he always left early, even though this was a well-known fact, no one could prove it. Phillip started to talk as his dad sat there smiling, he was all dressed up in a silk suit, he was showing his pride as he winked at his son with a big thumb-up. Phillip made the remark that his dad was no doubt the fastest man alive, stating that he got off work at five o'clock and was home by four o'clock. Phillip won the bike, but his dad lost his job.

Pin the Tail on the Donkey

Growing up on a small farm with six sisters was quite a challenge. Every family back then had a lot of children. It was just like Aunt Hazel said, "Good thing the community has nothing to offer in the way of entertainment. If it had, a lot of you youngsters wouldn't be here today." At the time I was only six years old and didn't understand what she meant.

In the spring of 1951 Mother went to her sister's place in Clyde River to nurse her back to health after her fall down the cellar steps with an arm load of wood for the furnace.

Gramma took over Mother's duties at home and every Saturday night was a dreaded bath hour. We didn't have a bathtub so we had to stand in a foot of warm water in a copper wash tub. Gramma would take a sponge and start washing our feet, then she would say, "I'll wash up as far as possible." Then she would wash our heads and say, "I'll wash down as far as possible." Then she would hand us the sponge and say, "O.K., now you wash possible."

One day at school we were playing pin the tail on the donkey. Our teacher had to leave the room but told us to continue our game quietly. Soon the jolly janitor came in like always to empty the trash can. Every time he bent over, being a large fellow of four hundred pounds, his trousers would slip down a bit and unintentionally half-moon us.

As fate would have it, Diane Davis was blindfolded, with the donkey's tail containing the shiny sharp thumb tack. Just as the poor janitor bent over to retrieve the wastebasket, he was mistaken for the donkey. Diane later said she knew something was wrong when she felt a vigorous quiver.

Screams filled the air along with two pounds of discarded paper. Diane started crying as the startled custodian made several rear end swipes at the tack that he thought was a bee. Us kids went out of control with laughter as the teacher rushed in the room to discover our outburst. We had to spend the next five recesses inside and write individual apologies to the janitor.

On our walk home from school we noticed a lot of people entering the courthouse. Our sheriff, who held the record for the most double chins, had Dirty Louie in handcuffs. Apparently the folks were tired of him giving our town a bad name; he never changed his clothes, ever exclaimed Aunt Hazel. The judge asked Louie how often he changed his shirt in a year's time. Poor Louis paused then said, "Oh, at least twice. Why judge, how often do you switch yours?" The old judge looked indignant as he rumbled, "Ha, once a day, sometimes twice if it's hot."

Louie ripped back, "Then how for the love of Mike can you call me dirty when you soil more than three hundred and sixty-five to my two."

That did it, Louie was sentenced to a bath and the two in turn would buy him a dozen sets of new clothes. Aunt Hazel was considered out of order as she jumped up and shouted, "Why in tarnation should we have to buy old mister filthy here clothes. I demand this a bunch of nonsense and purpose that we buy him absolutely none."

Old Louie leaped up in defense and yelled, "I second the proposal."

Aunt Hazel was a tuff ruff old gal who was very tidy, kept herself up well but had a serious problem with her food chute. She couldn't keep a secret, no way or no how. Uncle Ed got so mad at her one night at the dance he shouted, "Hazel, loose lips sinks ships." She took offense and traded his remark with one of her dreadful Karate chops. Dad later said, "I thought he might starve to death bouncing."

A few weeks later the word went around town that there would be a meeting at the town hall. Everyone seemed to be there, even us kids were invited. Seems that a circus wanted to come our way, so to insure a full house they wanted our response. The town folk were overjoyed and voted unanimously in favor of the idea. Now they asked us kids our thoughts, some cried, others said no way. The adults were troubled and puzzled. They asked, what, no circus, why don't you want to see the clowns and elephants, lions and the big cats, why, why? I shed a big tear and shyly said, "'Cause Aunt Hazel said if our community got entertainment, us kids wouldn't be here." Aunt Hazel covered her face and hurried from the hall.

Ski Jump on a Bicycle?

Harry was twelve years old and I was ten at the time when we decided to take a five-mile bicycle trip to a winter resort called "Beaver Dam." The year was 1955. Mom packed us a lunch for the long journey and Harry shoved two chocolate candy bars in his pocket for quick energy.

After peddling up hill for two miles, we stopped for a rest. Harry started bragging about finding the two candy bars that his parents had hidden and how he accidentally found them while looking for his Mickey Mouse wrist watch, which today would be very valuable. He handed me one, which was quite a treat. We very seldom had candy except for fudge that Mom made once or twice a year. We finally finished our delightful snack, so off again we peddled.

We didn't get very far before I took some sharp belly cramps. I had to stop and tight leg it to the nearest brush. Harry also did the same a short distance up ahead. We both were marking some healthy grunting sounds as I yelled to Harry asking him the brand name of those candy bars. I could hear him faintly unwrapping the paper, then gave a shout "Exlax." After awhile of having a rest stop, if you want to call it that, off we went heading to Beaver Dam. We were excited to get there. This being August, we were aware that the place was closed down but the vacant ski slope was enticing. We peddled around the place exploring the buildings and etc. Now I noticed my back tire was flat, so I leaned my bike up against a tree. I seated myself on the handle bars of Harry's old overloaded vehicle as he strained to peddle us around.

We made our way to the vacant ski jump and glared down the steep slope. Harry tried to scare me and he did, when he eased the bike's front tire toward the steep edge. I yelled at him, while still sitting on handle bars, that he'd better back off, we were inching too close. Harry chuckled, little did we know that would be the last one for a long time.

I was a fat little guy, so my weight on the front of the bike demanded too much on the front of the bike as Harry tried to jam the worn-out brakes. Terror set in rigor mortis, as our death trip took off in high gear. We took turns screaming as a funny noise arose from the back end of the speeding bike. I soon realized Harry was expressing his concerns from

both ends, thanks to the Exlax and all. Tears streamed from our eyes as I thought, "This must be what it's like to do a hundred miles an hour." Knowing we were half way from the big jump, we again screamed—this time in unison. It must have been loud because a woodcutter later claimed he heard us over a mile away. I had landed fifty yards from Harry, after Dad received the news, Mom and him arrived and took us in for medical attention. Harry broke his arm, I broke a leg, but Aunt Hazel said we were lucky because Harry's bike looked like a wad of gum, and even today it might still be up there.

The years have flown by since then, I had a letter from Harry awhile back stating that he now owned a beach buggy and this summer when I come home on vacation he said we could take it up to Beaver Dam. Then he wrote, "P.S., I'll have the brakes up and working by then. Your Friend, Harry."

The Bear Is Back

The most important season in remote parts of Canada is fall. Canning fruits, vegetables and smoking fish is a must if one desires to make it through the harsh frigid wild winters.

When I was a kid growing up, it was a fun time also. We used to net a fish we called a kayak; they would migrate from the Atlantic Ocean to the rivers and spawn. Dad would smoke three or four hundred at a time using poplar wood shavings for the fire.

The smoke house was a square building with wooden racks, no windows, just a thick door to keep out the hungry black bears.

I remember one night in late October us kids was sleeping when our dog Nipper started barking at something outside. Dad grabbed the rifle and rushed out to find the problem. However, he wasn't gone long when he rushed back in yelling something about "three toes," a huge black bear. He grabbed a higher caliber rifle along with a lantern and tore towards the smokehouse. Us kids ran downstairs to Mother as she gathered us around her. Then we heard two loud gun shots and a horrible scream. Father bounced in the back door without opening it as my little sister started crying. Mother ran to his side as Dad lay on the floor gasping for air. It seems old three toes had busted down the smokehouse door and helped himself to the smoking kayaks. Dad was really concerned now because he thought he had wounded the beast just enough to make him mean and vicious.

Us kids could no longer go out after dark and the whole neighborhood was terrified big time. My Uncle Ed and Dad set huge traps all around the smokehouse but old three toes would rip them away as his lust for the fish grew more intense.

The hunting party grew to a dozen or more but the old three toes was elusive and very clever. Everyone dreaded to see night time, that's when he struck the most.

One morning my friend Harry and I was playing outside the house, I happened to look down and noticed his foot print. On the left foot there was only three toes. Dad said he probably lost the other two in a bear trap when he was young. Late one afternoon the hunters returned. One of Brad Perry's hounds was torn up pretty bad when he cornered old three toes in a meadow about three miles from our farm. I could hear the men talking on the back porch. They were giving up the hunt, old three toes was just too clever.

Next day at school my friend and I had a motive, and that was to capture the bear alive. The next day we borrowed two shovels and a pick ax from the barn, walked around the woods where the bruin was last seen. Finally we found a trail that was worn down from use, we were certain the user was old three toes. After clearing some brush away, we engaged our shovels and started digging a deep pit. We worked all that day, after school that week and the following Saturday. The pit was ready, six feet wide, ten feet deep. We retrieved the homemade ladder, covered the hole with small tree limbs and pine branches, concealing it as though it wasn't there.

Next morning we crept back to take a look, nothing! This went on the following week, but Saturday morning Bingo! Something had fallen into the pit making loud grunting sounds, Harry and I raced back to the house yelling for Father. He wasn't home so we relayed the news to Mom. She rang the big brass dinner bell, soon neighbors came running

as we proudly announced, "We caught old three toes." Everyone was trembling with excitement, Aunt Leafy started crying when she said, "You boys are going to get the biggest party ever!" There was sixteen of us going to the pit, Uncle Nic loaded his rifle along with three others.

Boy did I feel proud marching along, Harry and I had done something right for a change, wait till Dad gets the news, yahoo! Thinking about Dad, I asked Mom where he was, she rubbed my head while still walking and said, ". . . back here somewhere cutting firewood." Hearts hammered in our chests as we neared the pit. Uncle Nic turned around and said, "Some'uns in thar aright." He raised his rifle while walking closer, then it happened. A loud screaming voice echoed, "Get me out of here." Uncle Nic jumped two feet high, took off running mumbling something about a talking bear. Uncle Bob now crept to the pit, motioned me over there. Looking down, I expected to see old three toes but instead I seen my old dad. He was shaking mad, especially after I waved and said, "What you doin' down there?" He told me to stay right there as my uncles started helping him out of the pit. However, I disobeyed this order and took off running. Three days later Dad's sprained back was better. Old three toes made no more visits, Mother seemed to think that father's screaming while in the pit was too much for him. I agreed with Mother when I said, "I can understand that, I couldn't bear it!"

3

Three, Two, One, Blast-Off?

The most wonderful time in anyone's life span is the ages between three and fourteen, that's the way it was for my cousin Harry and I anyway. I remember the school days most of all, just like this one time when the teacher let us play pin the tail on the donkey. Then with a paper donkey's tail and thumb tack, we would try to find our target to pin it on. I remember it just like yesterday when Diane Davis, then six years old, took her turn to find the donkey. After the teacher spun her around several times and with a blind fold on, off she set. At the same time old Mr. Barkhouse the custodian entered the room to pick up the trash. The timing was right on, just when he bent over Diane stuck the tack in the poor soul's backside. His scream was sharp as his numb hand felt for the object that gave him such discomfort. We all laughed and so did the teacher, as he kinda hopped from the room with the donkey's tail awaving.

We also later on had a baldheaded man teacher, he was stern and the only time I saw him smile was one cold December day when he caught Willie in the face with a snowball. Thinking he was in a playful mood, Willie heaved one back along with the rest of us kids. He raced inside the school and so did we, along with the ringing bell. Once seated, he cleared his throat and said, "Children, because of your rude actions outside, all playground privileges will be lost for one month."

I think if Harry hadn't booed, he would have left it that, but instead he made it two months instead. This was terrible. The worst part of the whole thing was looking out of the schoolhouse window while he was outside building a snowman, knowing very well we were watching from the window.

Well, the winter passed and spring break was one day away. Old "chrome dome" again spoke up, telling us not to waste our time during the break but make some kind of important invention, then once completed he would come to our homes to take a look and grade it. If he found it worthy he would no longer take our recesses away for the remaining school year.

The next day we kids met by the lake to consider something to invent, but everything had already been invented so we played ball the rest of that day. After supper the sun set, then there was a big bright full moon. Something snapped in my head as I thought that Mr. 'J', our teacher, would enjoy a trip to the moon. Next morning us kids gathered again, I told them my thoughts, then Harry mentioned a cartoon where Mickey Mouse sent a cat to the moon with a huge sling shot. That did it, in no time at all we picked out a forked tree, then went to my Uncle Nic's scrap yard where we found several innertubes. My uncle was good to us kids, so we revealed our secret, then he cut the tubes and tied them together for us. Boy, we sure thanked him. All that day much labor went into the launch pad. We employed the old plow horse to stretch the rubber back, once there we tied it to a tree, made a comfortable seat with some straw and now we needed our astronaut, Mr. 'J'. Things looked good for the takeoff, clear sky and the full moon would soon appear, even the lake, which was only twenty feet away, seemed to sparkle with delight, as it made clean ripples of tiny wind waves.

Harry jumped on his bike, an hour later we could hear Mr. 'Js' old rattle trap coming up the dirt road. When he got out we all tried talking at once, excitement was in the air, so would Mr. 'J', but of course he didn't know nothing about this. We led him down the path to the launch pad. He didn't notice the straining rubber tubes, he just kept complaining about the long walk, and our invention had better be worth his trouble. When we set him in the cockpit he kept yakking about what was going on, we told him he was about to go the moon, he yelled, "That's impossible." We fitted him with a pair of antique goggles and an old football helmet, we actually thought we could put him on the moon, da-a!

Just as he tried to leave his seat Harry cut the mooring rope. The takeoff sounded like a face slap. The whip lash was so great Mr. 'Js' goggles and helmet flew off. We all looked skyward, but he went lakeward. Willie manned a rowboat and soon had the splashing astronaut to the shore. He wasn't sure what happened, he just kept spitting water. Word spread fast, soon he was in our house drying out by the woodstove. Soon he came to his senses; kept yelling threats at us kids. We noticed he had a postage stamp stuck on his tongue, then he started crying. Harry looked at me and said, "Back to the drawing board."

Thanksgiving in the Good Old Days

Thanksgiving was special to us eight kids in Canada in the fifties. Uncles and aunts would be there and everyone would stuff themselves and then sit out on the porch, weather permitting, and listen to Uncle George tell us stories.

I'll never forget this one Thanksgiving because we had one old turkey that Dad was to butcher. His name was Jake, us kids raised him from a baby. At that time we promised Dad if he would let us keep it until it was full grown we would let him butcher it for Thanksgiving. Well—that day

came but we weren't ready, so we hid Father's sharp ax behind the barn. Father asked me if I knew where it was. I didn't because I let Harry hide it, so I didn't have to fib. Father was angry as Jake gobbled a laughing tune. He tore off to the house and in seconds was back with a shot gun. However, Harry and I had this covered too. We took the lead shot from the shells so all was left was the powder. Father told us to stand back as he blasted away; Jake just flapped his wings and strutted around.

Father was really puzzled now, as Mother started yelling from the back porch. I also started yelling at Father but stopped suddenly as he glared at me, making me hush. I took off running and so did Jake. That afternoon things settled down. We were sure Jake would be safe now, for tomorrow would be Thanksgiving. All Jake had to do was make it through the day. This should be a snap because we had to go in the meadow to pick cranberries with Father. The big purple berries were plentiful so my sister Linda and I filled our bucket up in no time. We had our second bucket half full when we noticed Father had left. We looked at each other and took off running.

We made it to the big clearing when we heard a shot. Jake? We dropped the berries and ran towards the pasture and what I seen still hurts a bit even today. Father shot Jake! I was furious and with tears flying everywhere, I screamed things I probably didn't mean. Dad also had tears in his eyes as he hugged me and tried to explain that times were hard and there would be fifteen people for dinner tomorrow. He went on to explain that I had made a promise about Jake, and if I didn't keep my promise today then how would I keep it when I grew up? We talked for a long time, then I finally understood somewhat about the situation.

Father asked Mother for some help plucking and cleaning old Jake but she refused. My sister and I didn't sleep much that night so morning came quickly. I heard a rooster crowing to welcome a new day but the gruff gobble gobble could no longer be heard. I think Father had second thoughts as he sat on the door step with his head down, but like Mother said, a promise is a promise. Mother did her duty and soon old Jake was aroasting.

Aunt Jenny and Uncle George arrived along with all the other uncle and aunts. I brightened up somewhat when my friend Harry arrived, he was twelve years old and full of wisdom, so I told him what happened. He was very disappointed as he pulled out his turkey call, he had planned to talk to Jake. He made it sound just like a turkey.

Soon it was time to eat but when Mom pulled Jake from the oven all of us kids told Mom we weren't hungry. We were ordered to be seated anyway, as Father began to say grace. With all eyes closed and heads bowed Harry slipped under the table with his turkey call in hand. David said amen, picked up the carving knife and poked old Jake. Harry let loose with his turkey call directly under him! Father reared back with such force he went over in his chair landed on old puss—our black and white cat. Puss screamed, Father screamed, making a grab for the table cloth. Everything went flying, including old Jake. He smacked father in the face leaving a red burn spot on his forehead. Uncle George dumped a whole pitcher of ice water on Father to ease the burn. He leaped up from the floor covered with mashed potatoes and gravy; he tried to run for the kitchen but tripped over Jake. Harry let loose again with the call as Father landed on his butt, the greasy flood held no traction. The entire living room was a big mess as Mother held on her head repeating, "Oh dear Lord, oh dear Lord." Us kids shouted, "Way to go Jake!" We thought we were in trouble big time, but Father sat there on the floor, studied the situation, then started laughing as everyone joined in.

The mess was cleaned up, Jake was buried, then we went out on the porch and had cookies and ice cream. Uncle George cleared his throat and began to tell stories. I learned a lot that Thanksgiving Day as everyone ended up happy and laughing, and ya know, I believe old Jake somehow did too!

The Bridge Is Falling

Back in the Thirties, when Mom and Dad were married, it was a long ride or a walk home. There wasn't a bridge crossing the Roseway River so folks who lived up the road in Welchtown had to make a horseshoe around it to get home. Everyone complained but very little was ever done. It was a sad day when my uncle's house burned down. The chief from the fire department said if there had been a bridge, they probably could have saved most of the house, but because taking the long way around the horses simply ran out of steam. He also said that the outhouse was the only thing standing, and that's a pity, exclaimed Chief Pike.

It wasn't until the Forties, however, when work finally began on a big wooden bridge that would stretch one hundred and forty feet cross the river. Instead of hiring a bridge company, the town counsel decided to hire local help, insisting that the savings would be tremendous.

Grant Dofinnie, who owned the town quarry pits, was contracted for laying the foundation stones, but when he learned that he had received his bid, his jump for joy was too much weight for the soft pine floor. He soon found himself in the basement with a broken foot.

The morning finally came for the work to start. The mayor was to fire a shot gun shell off to signal this historic event, in doing so, Whit White, an innocent bystander was hit by the shot and the mayor was accused of careless conduct with a harmful weapon. Whit ended up with a glass eye, the mayor was on a jury trial, but the ruling was that Whit was insane and not accountable for the mayor's actions.

Mother said she had a bad feeling about the bridge when she was packing Dad's lunch for his first day working on this new project. Things went pretty good the next few months, then on July 22, 1945, the new bridge was completed. Now there would be a ceremony and a band would play as the ribbons would be cut by the mayor, and Welchtown's leading citizen, Ken Godsee, would hold the scissors on the south side and both sides would meet in the middle and shake hands.

It was a bright sunny summer day, as the band drummed in the still air, when the ribbons were cut, then both sides started their march on the bridge, as they planked their feet down hard, reassuring themselves that this homemade bridge was sturdy, as the paper called it. There were approximately two hundred folks proudly shouting their support as the mayor and Mr. Godsee shook hands. Unfortunately that wasn't the only thing that shook.

Most people screamed as the bridge tilted to the port side. Folks started shoving each other trying to reach safety, but then it broke in two, as the screaming grew intense. Some hung on and rode it down, others hit the water and swam ashore. Panic played a big part now, as screaming hit a good pitch.

It was late afternoon until everyone was ashore. Most had scratches and bruises but nothing serious. Trouble broke out immediately when Lib Chase pointed to Aunt Hazel, claiming it was her fault. Then the blame turned towards the men who built the bridge. All a sudden a free for all took place, and this of course was right up Aunt Hazel's alley. Dad said she looked like a wringer washing machine working as she hurled her former friends into the river, with a delightful grin on her face. The mayor grabbed the plank that had floated ashore and smacked Aunt Hazel across the back. It sounded like someone slamming a car door in anger. Aunt Hazel took chase, someone said he looked like a hedgehog trying to escape a grizzly bear. When she finally caught him, the terror showed on his face. You could hear the wind whistling through the holes in his teeth as she hurled him around by his feet. When he hit the water his body skipped three times. Being closer to the other side, he swam ashore, then ran a good distance and stopped, cupped both hands to his mouth and called my aunt an idiot.

A huge crowd gathered now on both sides of the river, they calmed down as they watched more pieces of the bridge flutter by. When a group of engineers later examined the spot where the bridge once was, they said that the south pilings had shifted, causing the wooden structure to collapse. In the early Fifties a new bridge of steel was built, everyone in town claimed it wouldn't last a year, stating that it was much too heavy. I got a letter from back home at Christmastime, it was a postcard with the same bridge in the background. After completion of the new bridge, the first one to cross was the mayor, he also was the first one to jump off, but everyone said that Aunt Hazel gave him a helping hand.

The Three Strangers

Every single time a stranger came to town the folks would get together and gossip about the purpose of their visit. Aunt Hazel said the minute he stepped from the bus she would stake her life on the fact that it was Baby Faced Nelson.

Most of the folks on our small community were hard working farmers, fishermen and granite workers. Most of the women were housewives with two or up to fifteen children. For entertainment, our town of two hundred and fifty folks held very little. The most exciting thing to do was watch for the bus each Friday, then watch for strangers to step off, then speculate what business they might have in our town.

The second man to put shoe leather on our street was tall and slim. Aunt Leafy identified him as Clyde. The beautiful blonde of course had to be Bonnie, then she slapped the arm rest of Dad's 1949 Ford claiming this statement to be a fact. It seems we were eager to keep legends alive back then and they never died off, no matter who might otherwise know different.

I remember three cars parked at the station, including ours. I was seven years old and trembled with excitement as I watched the supposed Bonnie and Clyde head to the town's only hotel, and behind them the coolest of the cool, Baby Faced Nelson.

Aunt Hazel leaped from Uncle Ed's car and started pounding on our windshield as she was radiant with gossip. She asked us to spread the word that there would be a town-hall meeting that very evening; there they would decide the best method to apprehend the three legends.

Father's car held six adults, but somehow on our journey to the meeting there were ten plus me. I was sitting on Uncle Bob's lap, Aunt Hazel was perched on Uncle Ed's lap as he kept complaining about her bony butt as he wailed in pain. We were packed in there like sardines, especially after picking up Sam Haderson along the road, who weighed about three hundred and twenty-five pounds. Father was having trouble steering the overloaded vehicle; every time he hit a pot hole someone would squeal in agony. Uh-oh, suddenly it happened. Someone cut loose. I was jerked around like a loose shingle in a hurricane as everybody except Sam struggled for the window handles. Father almost lost control of the auto as he screamed, "Oh boy, that one was right off the stack." Aunt Hazel piped up too and said, "I wish I had a cork, I'd put an end to that." Dad struck the binders as we all piled out into the fresh night air. After several minutes we were once again on our way, that is, all of us except Mr. Haderson.

When we arrived at the hall it was packed with busy bodies. My Aunt Hazel was chairman so she brought the meeting to order. She suggested that the town put up a reward dead or alive, however, a quick vote dismissed this proposal. Old Bert, the gun smith, who just got out of the slammer for arson, suggested setting the hotel on fire and smoking them out but the only fire he got to see was in the owner's eyes. After a couple of hours a plan was adopted which all agreed to.

Next day, Aunt Hazel dressed as a maid, knocked on the hotel door claiming she had clean towels for the bathroom, once in she looked around for any evidence that they might be hiding. Bingo, there on the table in big leters was a note which read, "Bank 8 A.M." As she was exiting the room she kinda bowed at the three some and said, "Good day Bonnie, Clyde and you too, Baby Face." The three just sat there with a strange look on their face, probably thinking she lost her marbles, no doubt. Once outside she raced to the waiting town folk and excitingly told them about the bank message she had seen. That did it, being almost seven thirty A.M., seven men made their way to the bank's roof, armed only with a huge salmon net. Aunt Hazel stayed below on the bank steps to signal the roofers when to drop the net. Sure enough, eight A.M. the three neared the bank's front steps, Aunt Hazel let loose with a sharp whistle, down came the net, over the three. Somehow Aunt Hazel got netted too, as the four screamed in confusion. Come to find out the three weren't crooks after all, they were surveyors from Halifax hired by the railroad. Everyone apologized to the strangers except Aunt Hazel, her attention was focused on a big black shiny car that pulled into the hotel's parking lot!

4

Hurricane Hazel Strikes Again

I think the most exciting thing in my childhood is when my Aunt Hazel got into boxing. We lived in a small town but it received a big name when my aunt beat two big well-known brutes known as the Bull Dozer and the other who went by the name of Whip Lash Jake.

I was twelve years old at this time and my Aunt Hazel was my hero. I seen her shirt sleeves rip wide open when she pressed a two hundred and fifty pound bar bell up over her head. Mother told us kids to stand clear when her temper flared. She would toss her Volkswagen around the backyard like a cat playing with a mouse. Her four-foot shoulders ran out of places to budge when she picked up stuff that a forklift would have trouble with.

I still remember the day when a messenger on a bicycle paid a visit to my aunt. She accepted a paper which got everyone's curiosity going. For several days folks would listen to gossip wondering if my aunt had received another invitation to a boxing match. That following week word got out that indeed my aunt had received another invitation, this time from a mountain of a man known as Obnoxious Ike. He hailed from Scandinavia but was the champ of Quebec for the past two years.

Talk ran wild around town. My aunt was huge but so was Obnoxious Ike and he had never lost a match, ever. The headlines boldly printed that no one had ever made it through the first rounds after stepping in the ring with Ike.

That following Saturday our town seen a sight that is still talked about in Canada today. Obnoxious Ike wanted to meet my Aunt Hazel at the town's frog and toad club. She eagerly agreed for an eight o'clock meeting, as folks ran high with excitement. I still remember that fancy car when it pulled into town. Folks drew gulps of air when Ike stepped out; he was a huge man and badly scarred up from his rough lifestyle. Poor Aunt Hazel. It was said that he outweighed her by fifty pounds, but she still was taller by two inches. That night they met right on time. Obnoxious Ike put his huge hand out and my aunt did the same, then he started to squeeze with all his strength, so my aunt did the same. Ike's legs started shaking, his road map-looking face took on a terrible expression as both knees hit the floor. It took three men to break the dreaded handshake, as ice was applied to Ike's crippled hand. His manager hurried him away as he left with some very undesirable words to my Aunt Hazel, but she just chuckled and said, "Don't be late next Saturday, Ikie old boy."

The week went fast. That next Wednesday chairs were hauled in from every school, bleachers from the ball fields and anywhere else they could find them. The ring was built with heavy lumber and the ropes were borrowed from a logging camp. The six acres on the farm was the place as trailers and cars started moving in. My cousin Harry and I received a whole dollar for helping out, we were so excited about the whole thing. We sometimes worked later for no pay.

Aunt Hazel would ride by every now and then on her bike that had car wheels replacing the original bike wheels, and her seat was from the old Farmall tractor. She was always chewing on something to retain the three hundred and fifty pounds of muscle. Finally the day had arrived. Obnoxious

Ike kept yelling things on how he would win, even the sports writers agreed with him, stating that Hurricane Hazel had no training. She was relying on brute strength and that dreaded left hook. My dad was talking to my uncle when I heard him say, "Hazel doesn't have a chance, this guy knows all the ropes."

My aunt was the underdog and the odds remained one hundred to one. Obnoxious Ike had the confidence of a wolverine and made some nasty remarks about my aunt. I still remember the first round bell. Obnoxious jumped up and hit Aunt Hazel so hard all her hair curlers were jarred out except one. Hurricane Hazel was moved back about one foot. Then my aunt made everyone rise up in terror. She put one arm behind her back then motioned for Obnoxious Ike to come over. This he did with great vigor and ready to knock my Aunt Hazel out. The slap could be heard in the next county. Ike forgot about that dreaded left hook so he slept well into the next day.

Everyone went crazy, my aunt was a super hero. She asked for no pictures. She was really upset, then she got down on all fours, crawling around the ring in the loose pop corn. Finally she stood up, asking my mom, who was standing close by, for her help to replace her missing hair curlers that Obnoxious Ike had knocked from her head. Then she smiled, faced the cameras and cried, "Bring it on."

The Bees Are Back

Our small community of two hundred and fifty people was depressed big time. Everyone was fond of honey but because of constant bear raids on the hives the bees got mad and left. Neighbors and friends, husbands and wives and even us kids were having withdrawals. Finally after a whole month without honey no one dared to mention anything concerning the desired sweet bee product.

Uncle Ed forgot one day and called Aunt Hazel a sweet little thing. The word sweet caused him a severe karate chop across the throat. It took three glasses of water before he could speak a word. Uncle Harry had to wear dark glasses for a week to hide his black eye, just because he called Aunt Goldie honey bunch without thinking. One of the town's biggest weddings was cancelled just because there wasn't any honey for the reception. Poor dad, he looked so sad. I told my cousin Harry that there must be something that we could do, but what? This one night my Uncle Nic got real romantic with his wife, Aunt Gladis. He started batting his eyes as he recited her these words:

Your eyes are blue and shiny, I love them when you're sad, but sometimes when you first awake they look like city maps.

Your hair is long and snarly and tangled in the back, but up on top its curly, why ain't it that way in back.

Your teeth are white and pearly except the one that's missing, reminds me of our picket fence, cause the gate is also missing.

Come here my little chicadee and sit upon my lap and let me softly tell you about the birds and bees . . .

Because of the word bees his bed didn't need to be made the next morning, but the kitchen chair was history way beyond repair. Next day my cousin Harry and I were walking to school down the long dirt road. When we approached Uncle Bob's place we noticed him nursing a huge lump on his noggin while still in his sleeping bag on his front porch. We didn't need to ask him what happened, all around there were demolished pieces of a rolling pin. That was entirely enough, we had to do something to restore peace in the homes.

37

Later we remembered a huge bee's nest across the lake hanging from an abandoned homestead. When Saturday morning arrived we met at the lake with a wooden pickle barrel that owned a strong lid. So in a row boat we went to the other side. We toted the old wooden barrel up by the shack and placed it directly under the swarming nest. I cut a big alder limb, trimmed it to the right size and quickly knocked the huge basketball-size mansion from its foundation as it plopped smack dab in the waiting barrel. Harry slammed the lid on as we ran and hid, giving the uncaptured bees time to calm down. Finally we were toting the barrel with our treasure toward the row boat.

Now what we didn't know was that the bees in the barrel that sounded like airplane bombers weren't the honey bees that dad desired, but instead was big stinging wasps. I couldn't help thinking how proud my dad and uncles would be, even the community might make us heroes!!

At last we were finally doing something right, honey would once again be part of our menu. I felt so good I almost cried. When we reached the shore from a distance I could see my dad and four uncles go into the cellar. Goose bumps ran up and down our spines. I told Harry, just think, we're restocking the honey bees, wait till Dad gets a load of these babies.

I squeezed through the cellar door and yelled, "Hey Dad, guess what I got for ya?" I felt myself slip on the third step as the old barrel bounced down and landed smack dab in the middle of the helpless pack as the bees tore from their prison. At first everyone froze, then it was Uncle Nic who took the first strike. Screams zoomed from within. Harry and I took off running as five desperate souls all shot out the door at once ripping it off as it if were paper. Dad sounded like he was yodeling, as he headed for the lake at neck breaking speed. Poor Grandpa's wooden leg flew off, but later Mother said he did just fine, even though he looked like a kangaroo hopping to water. Poor Uncle Bob took two rear end strikes while climbing under the haystack. Mother said next morning Uncle Ed's shoes were in the cellar still tied. Aunt Hazel said Uncle Ed ran a fever all night as he made dreadful bee sounds in his sleep.

Well, to make a long story short, my chores were doubled. Father made me stay close to the farm and real busy the rest of the summer. You could say, busy as a bee!

Everything's Coming Up Roses

Mike Crow was a mean old man, he even disliked us kids and was cruel to our dog Rascal. One day he put grease on our bicycle seats, then laughed when we got spanked by our parents for getting our trousers dirty. He even put glue on the seats in the outhouse one time, poor Grampa got stuck so bad my dad had to pry him loose with a pancake spatula. Gramma made the remark that the poor soul had to sleep on his stomach for almost a week.

When I was nine years old Mr. Crow made me a sling shot for my birthday. I hugged him for his kindness but broke out bawling when I pulled it back. He put the rubber bands on real loose so they flew back, slapping me half silly, as I staggered around holding on to my cheek.

Mother said one day at the old folks' home, somehow he got invited to Thanksgiving dinner. Apparently when no one was watching he stuffed an inflated balloon inside the turkey. Then when the guest of honor, who was one-hundred-year-old Jeb Turner, jabbed the turkey with a sharp fork, it exploded. Poor Jed jumped so bad that his glass eye jumped out, landing in the punch bowl. Anyhow, it took thirteen old men in their eighties to throw him out. Once outside he stood in the street. "I've been kicked into better places."

Somehow, that afternoon Mr. Crow returned to the old folks' home for revenge. My Aunt Hazel told it this way, with her hands in the choke mode. "The miserable thing came in the back door dressed up like a wheelchair repair man. It just so happened that very night they were going to have a wheelchair race, so naturally no one paid him much attention as he visited each of the old folks. But listen to this, the knuckle head loosened all the wheel bolts on each chair. It was sick, sick, and more sick."

After saying this she turned her head toward the wood stove and spit a silver dollar-size plug of chewing tobacco; we listened as it sizzled on the hot surface. After wiping her mouth she again bit off a chew, folded her huge muscle-bound arms, and continued on as she said, "Then the creep stood there watching those poor souls wheel their hearts out as the race began." Screams could be heard next door, as wheels rolled everywhere, some lost one, others lost both." And listen to this, minutes later it looked like the end of a demolition derby."

False teeth and silver wigs were all over the floor. "And thank God no one was hurt, that's all." Now my Aunt Hazel had made herself mad, rolled up her sleeves and while raising herself from the chair growled back, "Enough is enough."

Two hours later my dad and I was hoeing potatoes in the garden when we heard a siren way down the road. Dad leaned on his hoe handle and said, "Sounds like that's coming from Mike Crow's place." Later we learned my Aunt Hazel walked in his house and gave him a pile drive head first on the floor. The doctor told my dad that Mr. Crow had to unbutton his shirt to spit, and would be in the hospital several days.

He gave the nurses and doctors a real bad time, even sweet little Dixie, a nurse who everyone loved, started crying. Several staff threatened to quit, that is, until Aunt Hazel made a visit giving them an idea. Little Dixie told Mr. Crow they had to take his temperature, so he opened his mouth, but she replied, no, no, turn over and butt up. Mr. Crow refused, until the doctor explained that he couldn't leave until they took his temperature. Mr. Crow screamed back, "Yeah, who says?" The doctor replied, "That gal they call Aunt Hazel, that's who." Immediately he did what he was told. Dixie did her duty, as Mr. Crow lay there complaining every second. She somehow left the door wide open to his room as the thermometer continued to take its reading. Everyone passing by got a big laugh and soon a crowd gathered and roared until tears bounced off the tiled floor. Angered big time, Mr. Crow yelled, "Haven't you half-wits ever seen a thermometer before?" Someone yelled back, "Yeah we have, but not in the form of a long stem rose."

It's Christmas

The snow was ten inches deep and still coming down in glorious big white flakes. It was the Christmas season and us kids were thrilled when Dad hitched up the horses to the sled to find a perfect tree. The year was 1952, I was six years old but will never forget how happy we were that year and I will always hold it dear to my heart.

We lived on a small farm in northeast Canada in a big house Dad built housing eight kids. Soon Christmas Eve was upon us when Dad made the remark that we would travel six miles to town and deliver several gifts to a family who were in need of food and toys for their five young kids. Father got the curry comb out and groomed old Bright and Dime, our two spirited horses, fed them grain as us kids wondered what was in the bright wrapped packages as we loaded them into the sled. Soon we were seated as the horses whinnied in excitement to start the journey.

It was a dark night so Dad lit lanterns and fixed them to the sled as he clicked his tongue, snapped the reins as our sled ride began. If you have never taken a sleigh being pulled by two spirited horses on a dark snowy Christmas Eve night, well, you're about to! Everything comes alive—the smell of leather fills the air from the reins mixed with the warming barn aroma from the horses. The sled runners make a hushing sound as they dash through the snow, giving just the right pitch with the jingling sleigh bells. Our warm coats and fuzzy mittens give us the feeling of warmth and security.

I feel a love as I look at Father sitting there looking so proud as he glances a slight look at Mother, making sure she's aware of his ability to handle and control the two-horse-power sled. She looks up at her prince with respect and love as he pecks a tender kiss on her little button nose. Mother snuggles her head deep in his huge woolly shoulder. She giggles with glee as if she has been tickled on all ten toes. I see the steam from their breath as it dances skyward, getting lost in the fluttering snowflakes. I fumble over onto Dad's lap as Mom's warm lips kiss my cold ear. Dad hugs me tight and hands me the reins as he drums out with a loud voice, "That's my boy!" (I will always remember that moment.)

Seconds later we were blessed with a touch of heaven when we glided into the meadow. The northern lights put on a show with big blasts of flashing colors across the sky, which put us all in a state of astonishment. Our mouths dropped open as a mighty flash lit up the whole meadow, even the horses stiffened as if they knew something we didn't. Dad swung his arms across my shoulders and said, "Son, those beautiful brilliant lights are the glory beams bouncing off the crown of our Lord and Savior." We all softly whispered praise God. With a click and a snap off we rode in the winter wonderland. We blessed the family with gifts and hugs and arrived home late that Christmas Eve. Us kids felt so good inside, we not only gave but we received many memories in 1952, that kept coming back every single Christmas Eve.

Dad is no longer with us but every year at this time when I take my family with me to visit my mom I kiss her on her little button nose and I still see the northern lights in her smiling eyes. It's then I remember Dad's words about our Lord and Savior. Merry Christmas from Bud and his family.

Bug Huntin'

I was five years old in 1950, it seems the days were too short for me to accomplish all the deeds I needed to do. My dad would bounce me upon his knee, give me big hugs and call me his little smash. As you read on you'll see why I earned this nickname.

We had a very happy childhood with eight kids in all, but like all kids, mischief was very often hanging over our heads.

Novia Scotia has a lot of bugs in the hot humid July and August days. Lacking insecticides in those days us kids would make wooden hammers and go bug hunting. This activity pleased our parents and also helped keep down the insect population.

This one hot day Mother decided to have an outdoor picnic. I helped Dad set up the boards for the table, big rounds of pine blocks were used for the chairs as Mother made ready the hamburgers and hot dogs, etc.

Uncles and aunts filtered in along with some town folks, so around the table sat approximately thirty-six people. My pal Harry sat by me as Dad said grace. When he got to amen,

43

knives and forks were engaged, as chatter filled the gorgeous July day. There was only one problem, bugs!

Aunt Hattie was the first to complain, then Mother made a swat at a beetle and so did Miss Pearl. It was plain to see that this well-planed picnic had a few bugs, so I looked at Harry and we quietly slipped under the huge outdoor table with our wooden hammers. I never seen so many feet, first we played a little game of "guess who these shoes belong to?" I recognized Dad's right away; his big toe was sticking out of his worn-out cowboy boot. We recognized Aunt Hazel's also, size fourteen. Harry started to chuckle as he whispered, "Looks like snow shoes," then we both giggled.

Soon getting tired of this game, we got serious and began bug hunting. Soon Harry was on the trail of a huge black ant. Realizing he was being hunted, that ant would stop everytime, right on somebody's shoe, then look as though he was grinning, feeling safe and clever. We held our hammers up making ready for when he ran, just when we had him cornered the clever critter took a sharp left and headed toward Dad's exposed big toe. I tried to outsmart him when he was just two inches from safety. I let loose with a mighty whack, Dad jumped up with a terrible yell, as he leaped around on one foot. Mother helped him sit down as she ran into the house for bandages to wrap his smashed toe. I felt really bad as Father kept yelling stuff at me. He ordered Harry and me to sit at the table, and warned us to sit, eat and shut up! Soon the twisted look left his face, telling Mother the pain had eased. From the corner of my eye, I seen him get up, but he sure was favoring that sore foot. All of a sudden I heard a sound like thunder. Father clobbered me with a tin cookie sheet causing it to dent. Now instead of seeing thirty-six people I seen seventy-two. I grabbed for my Kool-Aid but my glass kept moving.

Mother started yelling at Dad about his actions, but he told her there was a bug on my head and apparently he missed. After a few minutes my vision finally focused again and things returned to normal.

Everyone was full as Mother cleared the table, Grampa took a lawn chair under the apple tree for a cat nap, as Dad followed suit. Most people went home after helping clean up so Harry and I started bug hunting again. Harry had ten bugs to my nine, that's when a dragon fly dropped in. I raised my wooden hammer as I chased him here and there. In no time at all we were under the apple tree, where Dad and Grampa lay snoring. Dad had a Bob Hope-type chin and wouldn't you know it, that bug lit right on it. Aunt Hazel used to tell us kids that if a dragon fly lit on your face, it would sew your mouth shut. I didn't want that to happen to poor old Dad so with a mighty whack I was even with Harry, as Father let out a terrible scream. Again, Mother came running as Dad's chin started swelling up. He tried to catch me, but his smashed toe and achin chin got the best of him. He was yelling all kinds of stuff at me, then dropped his head in his hands. I think he was half crying when he told Mother, "I'll be so glad when school starts, I'm so sick and tired of that fat little son of mine bugging me!"

5

Hurricane Hazel Versus Whip Lash Jake

We didn't want to act like nosy neighbors but our curiosity was at an all time high. I was twelve years old in 1957, lived on a small farm at the time, when a big fancy car pulled up into my Aunt Hazel's driveway.

Three well-dressed men bounced out and soon cameras were flashing when my Aunt Hazel opened the front door to greet them. She had beaten the big Swede in a boxing match, the one they call the Bull Dozer, now she was partly famous.

Mother told me to wander over there, to eavesdrop on the conversation, but act as though I was told to borrow a cup of sugar, that's all. My aunt wasn't fooled, she told me to go home and tell my folks that she was going to Halifax, Nova Scotia, to another boxing match against a giant they called Whip Lash Jake.

He was a heavyweight champ of Canada and had never lost a match, ever. Later that day we learned he had fifty-five knockouts to his record and no one would box with him because of this. My Aunt Hazel eagerly agreed as the slick promoter handed her pen with paper and she drew her 'X' on the dotted line.

Dad promised to go, which made us very happy, having the only car for our area, Aunt Goldie and Uncle Harry, my friend Harry Jr., and six of us kids, somehow would pile in. I helped Dad hook up the trailer, it was a four-by-eight foot dual axle with wooden racks. We watched it sink down as my Aunt Hazel stepped in it, as her four-by-three-foot shoulders rubbed the side. My young face twisted when I handed up her lunch, my arms met up with fatigue when her log-like arm reached down and fetched it up.

Off we started, I looked out the back window, my aunt was already eating her lunch. I thought how small that ten-pound ham hock looked in her big fist, as she chugged down a gallon of cranberry juice. The wind whipped her hair curlers around as her burp could be heard over the hot singing tires. Her huge head poked well above the trailer racks, as she bounced merrily up and down in her seven-foot-six-inch frame.

When we entered Halifax, it wasn't hard to find the Convention Center, signs everywhere advertising "Hurricane Hazel." Then we seen a poster of "Whip Lash Jake," he was living in Canada, but was a native of Afghanistan. He was fierce looking—he had a towel wrapped around his head and had only one tooth. My aunt was considered the underdog, didn't have any boxing training and many sports writers called it a suicide match.

The Convention Center was packed, cameras all over the place. Mom and Aunt Goldie went to the dressing room with my aunt, they tried to talk her out of it with every step but one hour later she stepped in the ring with her homemade boxing gloves and size sixty-two-inch coveralls.

The announcer grabbed the mike and announced "Whip Lash Jake," most people booed, but quit suddenly when he stomped his huge foot. Just before the bell he started laughing at my Aunt Hazel, called her a hick, then spit in her face. My aunt thought this was part of the game, so she spat back, only it was ninety-nine percent tobacco juice. Whip Lash staggered backwards searching for his vision, just as the bell sounded. Aunt Hazel's mighty fist looked like an airplane propeller spinning around. It was that terrible left hook that caught Whip Lash Jake—he ended up in the second row out cold. My aunt was a hero, she was awarded a big brass belt, along with five hundred dollars. The crowd went wild, my aunt was cheered and showered with hand shakes.

It wasn't until morning when we left for home from Halifax, once again my Aunt Hazel seated herself in the trailer. I again handed her up the twenty-five-pound lunch. Just before pulling out, Aunt Hazel asked the gatekeeper how her opponent was doing. His reply was, "Oh, not too good. He's flying back to Afghanistan tomorrow with a terrible whip lash, and on top of that, he's terrified of airplanes."

Solution for Unemployment

My dad surprised the whole town when he announced that he would be running for office in Canada, the year being 1949. There were two political parties known as the Tories and the Liberals similar to the U.S. with our Republicans and Democrats. We were Liberals at the time and unemployment was the main issue. Father gained the running name Sir Grant. On the Tories side there was a better educated man with the title Sir Lawrence.

We lived six miles from town on a rutty dirt road which was very demanding on our old Model A. We kids helped out with the advertising and nailed up signs—helping out any way we could. The town was also busy fixing up the Legion Hall where the big debate would take place next Friday night. Poor Dad was nervous and made many trips to the outhouse, which was newly remodeled, the seats were lined with raccoon fur to detour the cold. I remember how uncomfortable it was with the cold draft blowing up from underneath, but it was quite modern at the time.

Father practiced his crudely written speech night and day until he exclaimed his readiness. The day arrived and we told father how impressive he looked in his new coveralls until Mother noticed his worn-out wing tip toes were on the wrong feet. We were ready to go as Grampa tried to crank the Model A engine over but the compression caused it to kick back, spraining his arm as he leaped around trying to shake away the pain.

Us kids and six uncles and aunts piled inside the old car as Father grabbed the crank giving it a mighty whirl. The engine coughed to life but Father took off running for the outhouse. We waited inside the Model A with a chattering old engine shaking us to pieces. It was very dark outside when we noticed Father waving the lantern from the outhouse door. Poor Mom ran to him, then tore off to the house fetching him a set of clean clothing. Finally he ran to the car, got himself seated as another problem arose. When he snapped the headlamp switch nothing happened. He was very upset, worried about being late as Grampa beat on the burned out lamps. The only thing now to do was to light the two kerosene lanterns as Grampa stood outside on the running board and Uncle Bob with his lantern on the other side.

We started out but visability was only ten feet as Father squinted trying to see the road. We were sailing along quite well when Grampa yelled, "Halt!" It was too late, we felt the front end rise, then it dropped sharply and we screamed in unison. Father got a bloody nose as the Model A landed on two wheels. Everyone piled out holding onto their hurt parts. Bert the blue ox had bedded down on the road and even though we ran over him he didn't seem hurt. He stood there for a moment, shook his head, and moseyed off, disappearing into the night. We stood there awhile with Mom holding a handkerchief to Dad's nose as he told sister Linda to shut up her silly crying, and angrily hurled a large rock in the direction of old Bert.

Finally we were once again on our way and arrived just five minutes before the debate was to start. When we got there poor Dad took several deep breaths, then said, "Let's go in!" The room was packed but most impressive to us kids were the two radio stations they had set up. Dad walked around shaking hands trying to act like a politician as Mom sat there shaking her head. Everyone leaped in the air when the radio announcer plugged in his equipment, there was a big bang, then sparks flew over everyone as smoke struggled to the ceiling. However the second one burped to life as the meeting started after the windows were open to exit the electrical smelling smoke.

The debates grew intense mostly over the high unemployment issue. Sir Lawrence, the Torie, gave a lengthy speech about putting a bridge up over Clyde River so the trucks could haul lobsters and fish, tombstones and etc. to Halifax and Yarmouth. As it sat now most trucks only having six cycle engines could make it up over Lovers Mountain because of its steepness, this in turn according to Sir Lawrence would create more jobs. He finally sat down and got a huge applause. Father now cleared his throat and began his speech. He rambled on about this and that which didn't make much sense. Finally the crowd roared, "Yeah, yeah, yeah—but Sir Grant, what are you going to do in order to shorten the long unemployment lines?" Poor Dad, he scratched his head, squinting his mouth around like he was going to spit out toothpaste, drew a deep breath, and what he said put the lights out that night at the Legion Hall, "I'm going to shorten the lines by making them move closer together!"

Graveyard Nightcrawlers

The first day of trout fishing was only three days away. In Canada us kids could make ten cents a dozen by picking night-crawler worms. Willy was eight years old, I was ten and cousin Harry was twelve. Dad let the grass grow too high on the farm so it was tough finding the crawlers after dark. My dad mentioned that up the road five miles at the cemetery they kept the grass mowed and the worms was as thick as cousin Luke's head, Dad would often say.

That night there was a huge full moon, so the three of us jumped on our bikes and took off for the graveyard shift after getting permission from our parents. Willie's mom warned us to stay close by him, he was the nervous type and not only that, his Uncle Bunt just loved telling him ghost stories, especially on stormy nights. It was kinda fun, our buckets would rattle fastened to the handle bars and the old dirt road was easy to follow, lit up by the glowing moon. It took forever getting there but we made it. The yard was scary, especially with the squeaky hinges singing away as the night wind tossed the picket gate back and forth. We sat on our bikes for awhile watching the long shadows of the tomb-stones stretching across the yard, some thin, some tall, even some seemed to be moving. Harry broke the stillness when he softly whispered, "Come on you two."

Our faces loosened when we seen the shining worms laying by their holes ready to dive at a second's notice. You have to be fast and fast we were, 'cause in ten minutes we boasted two dozen night crawlers.

Things went well until a hoot owl raised goose bumps on our backs, then a big tree limb cracked to our right. Not knowing what broke the limb, we hid behind the large tomb, scarcely breathing. Willie started to cry, I tried to calm him down but seconds later a big crash sounded again, this time driving the three of us face down on the ground, so as not to be seen. Harry whispered that he was going to crawl up ahead to the next tomb and investigate. Poor Willie, he was terrified and begged Harry not to leave but despite his efforts Harry crawled away. Now is when things got spooky. I looked down the road and could see a tall figure walking towards us in the moonlight.

There was a rumor going around that ax head Jack was still roaming around at night looking for his head, which was detached in a logging accident some fifty years ago. My heart started racing, then Willie seen the figure too. I put my hand over his mouth to muffle his scream then whispered to him that it was Harry trying to scarce us. Willie started crawling toward where Harry was supposed to be and to his terror there was Harry. This time Harry covered Willie's mouth. The figure we seen was Sam Davis, he lived down the road aways, he also was looking for night crawlers but at the time we didn't know it was him, we were just totally convinced that it was ax head Jack.

When Sam seen the three bikes he thought maybe some graveyard mischief was going on, so he started crawling too. I whispered to Harry to crawl in a straight line for the gate then we'd get on our bikes and take off. Closer we got to the road the faster we crawled, we were really moving around a tomb when, smack'o, right head first into Sam. It sounded like two bowling balls colliding. Harry screamed, I screamed and Willie had an accident in his pants. We were still scream-ing as we mounted our bikes, and in a second we were ped-dling like a windmill. Willie's seat was slippery, he was crying but kept up the pace. At one point going down a steep hill, Willie passed us, phew, he was really loaded. Finally we ripped into our driveway. Father was just coming out of the outhouse, on his way to bed. We all tried to talk at once about ax head Jack. Dad told us to get in the car, we would go up there to straighten this thing out, that is all of us except Willie, he had an appointment with the bathtub.

Well things got back on track. Dad talked to Sam, but word got around town about our experience, now the word night crawlers took on a whole new meaning!

Cowboy Way

Carl was an old cowboy from Wyoming, he lived in Tillamook all through the fifties and sixties. This one day in

October he invited Rod and myself to his place up on Chance Road, to hunt deer. His hands were raw and his fingers were curled, caused from breaking horses in his younger days, according to townsfolks.

We arrived at Carl's place one hour before dawn. His driveway was a long gravel road, at the end was Carl's house, close to the Trask River. His dog announced our arrival. Soon the figure of a tall lean old cowboy appeared in the doorway. He was dressed for hunting except for his feet, he was barefooted. He ordered us inside and demanded that we eat breakfast with him. He exclaimed in a Western old drawl, "We are havin' biscuits, eggs and bacon the cowboy way."

We noticed his hands were dirty and the frying pan had never seen dish soap, but not to hurt his feelings we agreed to chow down with him. Carl's eyesight was very poor, that's why he poured maple syrup in the frying pan instead of oil. Smoke boiled from the old wood stove. Rod and I rushed outside for fresh air, right behind us came Carl and his smoking frying pan. We could smell some kind of odor, so our attention swung towards Carl—his thumb fingers were smoking from holding onto the hot frying pan. We yelled at him until he dropped the hot pan and developed another problem, he caught the dry grass on fire. In no time at all flames were wide and high. Rod got the garden hose as I raced to the river with an empty paint bucket. After an hour the fire was out. The worst was yet to come.

We wrapped Carl's hands in gauze and ointment, afterwards we opened every window in his house to drive out the choking smoke. We told Carl that we would give him a rain check and come back tomorrow, but Carl wouldn't hear of it. So around ten A.M. we started our walk through his pasture, hoping the deer weren't all spooked. Carl was still wobbly on his feet, so when we came to his electric fence a great deal of care was taken. Rod and I crossed alright, but Carl ran into trouble. When he straddled the hot fence his legs gave way, he started yelling in a high pitched voice. We tried to help him as his trousers began to smoke. His screams were deafening, as terror took us over. I grabbed his huge hand and started pulling but I got shocked too, so bad that I had to get loose. Rod came running with a tin can he found on the ground full of water, threw it on Carl to cool the high-pitched yodeling cowboy down. Well, it just made things worse.

Finally the wire broke and so did Carl. Rod and I helped him to his house, even though we realized he required much more energy now than before. Rod whispered, "That's because he got juiced." After sitting around the table for a spell, Carl asked me about my hunting vest, I told him the pattern was antique and went back to King Arthur the Second. Poor Carl, he felt really bad as he patted me on the back and said, "Son, don't feel bad, see that new TV over there that I can't pay for, well partner, let me tell you, that goes back to Sears the tenth."

We told Carl that we didn't want to hunt anymore that day, that's when he made a remark about his drift boat that was lying upside down out there in the field. He talked us into going fishing for salmon in that dry rot old tug. Carl outfitted us with fishing poles, so with quick prayers we pushed out in the Trask River currents. We hit a good spot to fish so Rod dumped out the anchor, but when the rope came taut, the entire bow ripped off the grandfather drift boat. Carl was holding onto the bow for dear life, as Rod and I drifted down the stream in the stern. Our cries for help brought some fishermen from downstream as we yelled back to Carl that we loved him, knowing that we probably wouldn't see him again. Rod and I were rescued but no sign of Carl. Some searched way down in the tide water, others probed the bottom with their oars, but no Carl.

We felt like crying. Carl was a mite crazy but we liked him a lot. Soon the Tillamook Rescue arrived as the search went on into the night. Then at dawn a lean figure appeared on horseback. When they got closer it was clear that Carl was alive. We asked him how he got ashore. Old Carl just pulled on the brim of his big Texan hat, smiled and said, "It's the cowboy way."

6

A Real Catchy Tune

It seemed every time our family enjoyed a stretch of good and happy times, a series of troubles would follow and upset the apple cart. My dad had a hard time adjusting to a new lifestyle in the U.S. after moving from Canada. He would often put his foot in his mouth after pretending he knew just about everything about our new town in Weymouth, Massachusetts.

I remember one day when he and I were walking downtown when a carload of tourists stopped and asked my dad where they might find a good restaurant. Dad didn't know but in order not to look bad he said, "Go about two blocks and you will see a big blue building on your right, nobody goes there anymore because it's always too crowded." Well, there was a big building there alright but it was a clothing store. One other time folks stopped and a conversation started about how nice our town looked, then out of nowhere they asked Dad what the population was at the time. Poor Dad, he kicked some leaves around, apparently stalling for time, he really had no idea, when he said, "Five hundred and five." He only missed it by five thousand and three hundred.

The Dick Van Dyke show was one of Dad's favorite TV series, on one show Laura and Rob, the stars of the show, came out on stage doing a duet about their boss, Allan Brady. They would sing "Al-lan Brad-dyyy, Al-lan Brad-dyy, over and over again, using high and low pitches in their voices. Somehow the catchy tune got stuck in Dad's head, and he kept singing it over and over, the poor thing couldn't even get to sleep at night, so then it became a medical problem. Mom made him a doctor's appointment and being a close knitted family the whole bunch of us kids went along. The doctor's secretary asked Dad his name, he shouted, "Al-lan Brad-dyy." She gave dad a sharp look, then she looked at us kids. We all had peanut butter and jam smeared across our faces from a quick lunch, then Mother piped up and explained the situation. Dad was taken back to a room where the doctor would examine him. We sat in the waiting room flipping through magazines, when all of a sudden we heard Dad's voice singing "Al-lan Brad-dyy, Al-lan Brad-dyy." He was singing it loud and clear. The doctor rushed in to where Dad sat, and things went kind of quiet. After a short time the doctor popped out and he too was singing the lively tune along with my dad. The nurse led him back to his office, but he continued singing. Dad joined him again in a different pitch, as they both sang their hearts out. The secretary radioed the hospital, which was next door, and asked for help. A well-known doctor who dealt with head problems was sent over. Poor Mom, she started wringing her hands, then started crying when that doctor too walked out singing the catchy tune. Father finally came forth. We left for home as both the nurse and secretary waved good-bye while they also reared back on the Allen Brady tune.

Next day the doctor's office called. They suggested that Father's problem was like a stuck record, and a good whack on the noggin might be the ticket. When Mom told Dad the news, he wanted no part of it, as he again sang the now dreaded tune. I couldn't stand it any longer, even the cat gave him a nasty scratch across his rosy cheek. Next day, Dad arrived home early from work, his boss closed shop as the entire crew of eight was infected with the Brady disease, as they called it. When he sat down I grabbed the rolling pin, which Mother had left out in plain sight. I tiptoed up behind him and let loose with a healthy whack. He jumped up and twirled around three times, his eyes looked weird, then he staggered towards the sofa and bedded down. You talk about happy, he was sleeping good, but no more Allen Brady was heard.

Our life returned to normal, Mom refused to let Dad watch that show anymore. He took it very well. About three months later he was watching Gunsmoke, then an advertisement came on the screen where a bread truck driver appeared singing "Williams bread, the good bread, flavor beyond compare." Father's lips started moving, Mother leaped up and unplugged the TV. I ran for the rolling pin, but was disappointed when Mom threw up her hands and said, "Hold it son, he didn't have time to catch that one." I handed her back the rolling pin reluctantly. I wanted to whack him again, just for good measure.

Look at the Long Line of Geese

Mother said it was terrible, no one could sleep well because of the feud that was going on for twenty-five years. She said it all started one day when her father went goose hunting with Chief Burbine, a native Micmac Indian. Chief Burbine wouldn't shoot the long side of the V-shaped geese flock. He told Father the left side were his friends who joined the flock of geese at the time of their death. Henry, Mom's dad told him he was crazy and the reason one side was longer he exclaimed was that it was surely caused by seniority. The less experienced birds flew on the left side, thus causing a longer line.

Old Chief Burbine was eighty-eight and had lived in the Maritime Provinces for all those years. He was a real respected Indian and his wisdom was sound, but our townfolk in Novia Scotia, Canada, couldn't accept his reasoning. They favored old Henry's idea which brought trouble from the tribe on a bright moonlit October evening. The tribe shot arrows at the Legion Hall where a town meeting was taking place. Mother said the old chief was so mad he told the mayor that he was going to scalp someone, but he was just about blind and couldn't find the door leading inside the hall. However, he did make it to the porch, grabbed the mop that was leaning there, then thinking it was a person, he drew his knife and ran from there yipping and barking, waving the mop head thinking he had a human wig. The fighting went on until morning with only some bumps and bruises along with a few black eyes, but things cooled off when the Mounties arrived from Halifax.

Old Henry wouldn't change his view of the geese, and neither would the chief. Just when we thought peace would never come to our town my dad, only twenty-five years old at the time, called a meeting making a statement that he was going to Halifax for two weeks. He said some big shots were there spending some three hundred thousand dollars of Canadian money to study why one side of the geese was longer than the other. He would be there making sure he had all the facts and he too would be working on the goose experience alongside the scientist. My mom and I said good-bye along with most of the townsfolk, as my dad boarded the bus.

The whole Micmac Indian tribe were there also, beating on their drums insuring one and all that the old chief was right all the time. I was only three but I could remember black smoke pouring from the bus as it chugged out of town towards Halifax with my dad throwing kisses from the window.

Time flew by. Soon the bus arrived after two weeks, we were there early to greet it and so were the hundred and twenty-seven Micmac's. Old Henry was walking around telling the folks how smart he was and he was about to pop a button from his shirt, as someone yelled, "Here she comes!" Mother started crying, not only happy to see Dad, but now the feud would end, and each one agreed, no matter which one was right it would be accepted and the book closed on the goose issue.

After the hot bus quit making its weary noises, Dad stepped out. You could have heard a pin drop, as he scurried up to the live mike. The mayor asked him if the scientist had found an answer. Dad smiled big, stuck his thumbs inside his pant pockets, leaned towards the mike and said, "Ahh, ahh, they say the reason why one side of the goose flock is longer than the other side is because there's more geese on that side." Everyone froze.

Roads, Rocks and Honey

In the early fifties our small town was growing by leaps and bounds. The saying at the time was "time and tide waits for no man." A small community was being built not far from where we lived, but the dirt road leading to it was so muddy and rough over half the traffic would get stuck and the folks would ruin their nice shoes trying to walk out there.

It brought great excitement when we learned of the new roads that would be built, therefore creating many new jobs. My dad and four uncles were hired, along with ten others, to build a rock road into the town known as Birchtown. It was hard work. Dad would come home at night with blisters on his hands then look at me and say, "Son, stay clear of pick axes when you grow up."

Things went well, Dad got paid ten dollars a week. It kept food on the table and the wolf from the door, but after the first month things started to happen. According to Dad there was an old woman named Pearl, she lived only inches from where the road would run. She came out one morning with a shotgun and three mean dogs. After demanding that the road crew turn around and 'get', she fired her double fired shotgun, blowing out the head lights off the old 1953 Oliver tractor. The crew scattered like rats. When they got back to town, Pearl was reported to the sheriff. He listened to the terrified laborers as he chowed down on a lunch which Dad said belonged to a fellow called Nick. He was real slim and didn't need to miss a meal. His nick name was two steps, he was so thin he had to take two steps before his pants would move. After devouring the starving man's meal, Sheriff Sam wiped his mouth on his sleeve, grabbed his billy club, then turned his three hundred-pound body towards Pearl's place. The road crew pleaded with him to be careful, but he just laughed and said, "I'll fix that old bat." Exactly one hour later they spotted Sam staggering towards them. His screaming was dreadful, and it looked like he had a tail, but once getting closer it was confirmed that it was a pitch fork stuck in his rear end.

Dad said he was soaked with sweat, but the doctor later said, it was boiling water that had been thrown on him. Enough was enough, the men was out of work for three straight days, so the following morning they armed them-selves with ax handles and went after Pearl. She was lean as a pole, and mean as a bear. No one knew much about her, she was seldom seen in town but had the reputation as a good rock thrower. When the crew got near Pearl's place the hearty talk ceased, their pace slowed. Dad was the foreman, so they made him go out first. He hollered out, "Pearl, we're gonna teach you a lesson." No one seen the rock, but it caught Dad right between the eyes, as he hit the ground with dust flying everywhere. Somehow he got to his feet and took off for town, the others followed on a fast run, but poor Uncle Bob lost the seat from his trousers to Pearl's mad dog.

The Mounties were called in but declined to help. They said it was a civil dispute, therefore they reneged any offer to help. Next day the road crew got a hold of Gib Guy. He was a good rock thrower, so they armed themselves with two buckets of rocks and headed to Pearl's place again. This time they decided to surround her house from a good distance and shower her hut with rocks. Gib stood up to throw the first stone but before he let loose a well aimed rock took him off the chin. He started running down the road crying, realizing this was a bad idea. The crew also took off running to town.

What were they to do? Sam made the remark about dynamite, but they couldn't get close enough to set it. That night a town meeting was called. A slick gentlemen named Ira McMay stood up and told the weary folks that they were going about the matter in the wrong way, and for a hundred dollars he would solve the problem and everyone would be happy, even Pearl.

Now Ira was a handsome lad, most folks didn't like him and kept their daughters far from his reach. He could sweet talk the meanest woman anywheres, and claimed Pearl was no exception. Realizing he couldn't get close to her shack, he tied a note to a rock and gave it to Gib to throw through her window. This he did, everything went quiet, then Pearl appeared and yelled, "You really think I'm cute?" Ira carefully walked up to her house, flattered her some more, and gave her a big smooch on her cold lips.

Well sir, the road went through, and the unexpected happened, Ira and Pearl hit it off and were married. He even brought her to town with him. Dad thanked him for what he did, then Ira winked and said, "Remember Grant, you can catch more flies with honey than you can with rocks." The road was completed two months later; they named it the Ira Pearl Highway.

The Talent Show

Fall was displaying her brilliant colors, geese winged south and everyone in Nova Scotia was getting ready for winter. This one year in 1953 I found myself on the other end of a crosscut saw. Being eight years old I was expected to cut my share of firewood. Wherever you looked wagon loads of wood was going every which way and it was just like Dad said when that old northern wind comes and snow comes awhipping we will be ready.

Now there were two men in their late thirties who rented a two-story house five miles from town in a place by the bay known as Sandy Point. The whole town was talking about how lazy they were, and it's like Aunt Hazel said, they ain't put a hand to an ax since they moved in. A big rumor was gripping the whole town and Aunt Hazel fanned the flame when she said it was true alright—the two men were from Hollywood and were searching our small town for talent. Everyone had their wood cut and stacked but old Will Fudd, who drove the taxi cab, made the remark that he was called to Sandy Point and talked to Wilbur and Earl, the two supposed talent agents. They made the remark that they would be spending the winter there, and yes they were talent agents but their wood supply was gone.

Dad thought he had talent because he could rattle two spoons together, making the sound of a lively step dancer. He decided to pay the men a visit taking a load of fire wood along for bait. When we arrived, half the town was there, they had trumpets, guitars, fiddles, banjos and old Gibbie Guy even had an old organ on a flatbed trailer. Some were stacking wood as others displayed their talent. Aunt Leafy sang a beautiful song called Harbor Lights, but choked half way through on a Life Saver. Uncle Bob displayed his dog tricks with Jack, an ill-natured bulldog. He ordered Jack to sit and talk but instead Jack sit and bit, this caused poor sister Joyce to run across the road to call a doctor.

When it was Dad's turn to rattle the spoons he found out that Earl was slurping soup with his instrument, which made Dad mad, but he politely retrieved it and made his debut. Evie and Ruth ruined the song, "Don't Sit under the Apple Tree with Anyone Else but Me." Poor Gibbie Guy climbed on his trailer, pulled out the organ stool and hammered out the tune, "'Twas the Night that I stole Old Sandy Morgan's Gin." He was half way through the joyful tune when the tire blew out on the pass-me-down trailer. The organ slid off, pinning Gibbie's left foot underneath. It took six strong men to free him, the doctor said he wouldn't be walking on it again until spring.

Everyone was getting mad, Earl and Wilbur didn't even listen to most of the talent, just sat there smoking cigars and tossing wood into the stove. Aunt Hazel again got everyone riled up when she said, "Ain't they something." Finally Earl stepped out, thanked one and all, and come spring he said, "You're all going to be on the Grand Old Opry." Cheers splintered the freezing night air, everyone was dancing and hopping around. A few days later the newspaper had big headlines "Twenty Stars Are Born." Well sir, the time flew by—soon the cold wild winter was finally gone, and so were Earl and Wilbur.

Was It UFOs?

The whole town was talking about what was happening. My Aunt Leafy was walking home when she was forced into a car by an elderly polite gentleman. She was driven to a house as the kidnapper demanded that she do his dirty dishes and clean the house, after which she was driven back to the exact spot and let loose.

I was just a kid and can remember how upset the whole town was, especially my Aunt Hazel. I was only six years old back there in Canada in the year 1951.

The mounted police questioned Aunt Leafy about the kidnapper and her experience, but she couldn't remember the right direction. She was told to cover her eyes and of course obeyed the order. Two weeks later Brad Perry's Model A Ford broke down just past the old bridge, when he got out to solve the problem, he was ordered into a car and forced to chop two cords of firewood. After completing the task he too was driven back to his fatigued jalopy and released. In each case both victims agreed that the abductor resembled George Washington, one of the early presidents of the U.S. Brad Perry also obeyed the order to cover his eyes and so indeed he too was of little help in the way of giving directions.

Us kids sure were excited when two Mounties on horseback started patrolling our old dirt road where both victims were abducted. Everyone felt safer now with the presence of the new law officers, that is, until they too were kidnapped as their horses wandered around the pastures aimlessly. Three days later they were released after building a horse shed.

My Aunt Hazel said, "Enough is enough, I'll catch this wise guy and put him behind bars where he belongs." Poor Aunt Hazel, I bet she walked up and down that road a dozen times but got no sign of a kidnapper.

Two months had passed without an abduction, so by now everyone was sure this crisis was over. Then on a Saturday morning trouble struck again. Lew Swaine arose from his sleep, ate breakfast, grabbed his milk bucket and headed to the barn to milk his old cow, Loliepop. Much to his surprise all that was in the barn was his blind cat Scat and his old milking stool. He leaped in his pickup truck and tore off for the sheriff, but a note "gone fishing" was all he seen, so he beats it up to my Aunt Hazel's place with his complaint. He entered the back door but had to wait till she put down her three hundred-weights that she was lifting to the count of twenty-five. Lew yelled uncontrollably about his stolen cow Loliepop. My Aunt Hazel put on her shiny badge along with a water pistol full of some kind of colored water. Mother said that badge of hers came from a Cracker Jack box but no one dared to tell her that except Ned Nelson, who stood seven foot two. Mother said Hazel's left hook was devastating as five of my uncles loaded Ned back on the wagon. He was out for two hours and for years later had trouble with his speech. The doctor also said his left eye would look like a peeled boiled egg. Anyway, two days later the cow was returned unnoticed, what was going on?

Aunt Hazel again walked the lonely road hoping to be picked up, but no sir. Uncle Ed told the newspaper that no one in their right mind would pick her up, she looked like a wad of gum held up by two tooth picks. The day the paper came out with that statement he stayed with us two days to avoid a beating.

Harry and I this one day was walking the dirt road when a car we had never seen before pulled up. They were city slickers, that was obvious. The driver looked down at Harry and said, "Hey son, you're missing a shoe." Harry also looked down and said, "Oh no, sir, I just found one." We told Aunt Hazel about the incident and right away she started asking us questions. We told her they didn't mean no harm, just city folks.

A year went by and no more abductions, things returned to normal but Aunt Hazel wouldn't give up. She now claimed it was space aliens who were responsible, she also claimed to be an astronomer. She said that the brilliant star Arcturus of the constellation was about to appear that evening. The sky was unusually bright with shooting stars and the marvelous Northern Lights was putting on an impressive performance. My Aunt Hazel jumped for joy, she was sure we would have a visitor from outer space.

She ran in the house, dragged poor Uncle Ed from his warm bed and wrapped him in flashing Christmas tree lights. Then she drawed back her fists demanding him to stand there no matter what, with all his lights flashing. However, nothing came of it.

7

What's Your Nick Name?

When we were kids, curiosity played a big part in our everyday life. Living on a small farm miles from town we learned a lot of stuff by experimenting. Just like the day cousin Harry got his head stuck in a goldfish bowl. Mother told me to clean the cloudy water and replace it with clear river water, so I poured Pixie and Dixie, my plump goldfish, in another pan of water as Harry and I dashed to the river to fulfill Mom's wish.

I asked my cousin, who was nine years old, to hold the slimey bowl until I got settled on the rock where the water was the cleanest. Harry, he was trying to fit the glass container down over his head, realizing his noggin was a mite bigger, he really started pulling. Seeing he needed help I slapped both hands down on the bowl, then I heard a loud pop as his head slipped inside. We both laughed at first, but panic drifted around a bit when we tried to remove the tight-fitting bowl. The glass steamed up inside, until Harry's head was hard to see. His bawling sounded like mini bumblebees. I couldn't help laughing. I pulled and pulled as Harry started bawling louder.

Then all once he took off running for the house. I seen Mother hanging out clothes on the line, so I guided Harry her way. Poor Mom, she threw both hands to her head as she cried, "Oh no!" She rushed him in the house and smeared butter all around the edges of that goldfish bowl, but still it refused to budge. My sister ran to the barn and motioned Father to the house. Poor Harry, he sure was in a fix! My dad tried everything but nothing worked, even the hammer was useless on the thick glass. All of a sudden my Aunt Hazel filled the doorway. She was the one who could solve most problems and there was no doubt Harry had one.

After about an hour, somehow she removed the steamed up bowl to the delight of everyone, especially Harry. The next day at school everyone heard about what happened so Harry ended up with the nickname "Jug Head." Even today that name still sticks. I received a letter one day from Harry and after almost fifty years that nickname hasn't changed. Cousin Willy took on the nickname "Stinky." I'll write about how he arrived at that name later, but I heard last year he was thrown out of the lunch room at work, after forty-five years that name still sticks.

A Family Feud

According to Mother, Amos Cunningham threw the first stone across the river, hitting Bill Durkee in the head, knocking him out. This was back in 1902, from then on the family feud swung into gear.

The Roseway River was a hundred yards wide and on the west side was the Cunninghams and the Davis's. On the east side were the Bowers and the Durkees.

Every Saturday afternoon the rock fights would start. Mother said folks on both sides of the river hardly ever seen each other because of the heavy brush that they would hide in as rocks flew all around them.

One day I got to go on the rock war even though I was only ten years old. First Dad and Grampa would hunt for rocks, the flat one-pounders were nice Dad said, they sailed good and was easy to hurl. My five uncles showed up, each toting a bucket of rocks. Along with Dad and Grampa there were three cousins, me and Aunt Hazel, who was our hillbilly country doctor, which made a total of twelve. I was sure excited to be there. Dad ordered me behind a big stump as everyone got ready.

Grampa would start things up by yelling rude things to the other side. But Durkee, son of Bill Durkee, had a wife whose name was Diareea Durkee, they called her D.D. for short. Grampa would yell, "Hey Burt, how's your Diareea doing?" I still remember the sounds of the whistling rocks as the Durkees and the Bowers opened fire. Grampa would laugh and then head for cover. Rocks were flying through the trees from both sides. I watched as they hit the stump in front of me, tree bark and leaves flew everywhere from both sides. The war would go on until someone got hit a serious blow.

Aunt Hazel was hiding behind a stump ten feet away. The whistling smashing rocks sounded dreadful and terrifying, everyone was yelling from both sides, it was really frightening. After about an hour it happened. Grampa stood up to hurl a rock when we heard a loud smack. He tried to keep his balance but his legs wouldn't stand for it, down he went. Dad put the white pillow case on a long pole, waved it high in the air signaling that the other side had scored a hit. Then the rocks stopped as Dad started yelling threats across at the Durkees and Bowers, letting them know that next Saturday they would even up the score. One of them yelled back bragging that one of the Durkees named Clarence was eight foot tall and was the greatest rock hurler ever. Aunt Hazel bandaged Grampa's head, then she picked up the scoring rock, which was in two pieces, tossed them down while making a comment about the thickness of Gramp's head, talking about rock on rock.

That night our team gathered at the house. They swarmed around Grampa laughing so hard tears seeped from their eyes. The poor old man was so delirious he was talking out of his mind, saying things about his private young days. I got to admit, it sure was funny. After tiring of that, Dad rolled up his pant leg, pointing to a rock scar. Then cousin Billy wiggled his left ear, which was cauliflowered big time, from an estimated ninety mph flying rock. Everyone was proud of their cuts and scars. Show and tell went on until late that night. The rock fights went on for five more years. Everyone was hearing the name Clarence, they talked of how tall he was, and pretty soon his name was a dreaded sound every Saturday afternoon during the rock fights. Our team took some big hits, oh yeah—from Clarence.

One day in early summer the county engineers decided to build a bridge across the River. When Dad heard the news he began to brag that when the bridge was finished he was going across and hit Clarence with so many rights he would beg for a left. By fall of that year the bridge was completed, Father told Mother the time had come to pay old Clarence a visit. Before he left Gramps gave him his old boxing gloves. Dad waved back as he made his way to the bridge. Mother started praying as Gramps hung his head thinking this might end the family feuds once and for all. Suddenly we heard Dad yelling for dear life, then he tore into the house out of breath. We rushed towards him, his eyes were big and wild looking. After a deep breath Dad looked up and said, "We're going to need bigger rocks, there's a sign upon the bridge that says, "Clarence is thirteen feet, ten inches."

Terror at the Cemetery

For you who would like to have more hair on your head, you should have been at the cemetery in Shelburne, N.S., Canada in 1952. It was a hair-raising event that took place. Old Clem was terrified of funerals and graveyards because when he was twenty years old he wanted to attend his uncle's funeral but wouldn't go inside the Church of England. Instead he sat on the bottom steps outside. Finally the pallbearers appeared with the casket as they struggled with the heavy cargo. At the top of the steep steps they started their slow descent, when all of a sudden the bottom fell out of the clumsy built coffin. Old Bert tumbled down the steps and landed smack dab on Clem's lap, still dead as a mackerel.

At that time they used to place pennies over the deceased person's eyes. Now Clem was staring straight at the two copper pennies, and making things worse the whole top of his head was some place else. Mother said the funeral parlor removed it trying to find out what made him tick. Poor Clem screamed so loud it spooked the horses that pulled the hearse wagon, then with all his might old Clem threw Bert in the wagon—as it took off in record speed racing out of town.

Clem was half out of his mind as terror took him over. He was running in circles, screaming and ripping his hair out, way out of control. However, this suddenly stopped when Mack, the funeral director, smacked him over the noggin with a "Keep off the grass"; sign that he pulled from the lawn. While Clem was counting stars the funeral people took off after their deceased client. Apparently the horses took a sharp turn on Eighth Street, whipping old Bert out as he slid into a packed donut shop. Two fat cops picked him up and tried to place him on the stool, not realizing his toe was tagged. They had him setting up pretty good when to their horror they discovered the top half of his head was missing. According to Mother they thought he had been murdered so they tore outside and apparently weren't thinking as they started firing their pistols at the first car they seen.

Anyway, the years flew by and old Clem was still having nightmares big time. When he was about half crazy his friends decided to drive him to Yarmouth to a shrink. He went under treatment for his graveyard fears and after six months of this they decided it was time to visit old Bert's grave. It had been forty years since old Clem had even been near a cemetery. So it took a heap of urging and probing to get him there. He was shaking like a wagon on a frozen road as twenty-three friends joined hands and sang hymns. Finally Clem nervously opened his eyes and stared at the mossy tomb stone. Friends patted him on the back as Lester, the ninety-eight-year-old pastor gave him a mighty hug—then in turn Clem gave him back a hug, while still facing the grave. Mother said, "I think it was the old devil that made that mole start pushing up dirt." Clem let out a rocket scream, right in the ear of the old pastor, then took off running, still hugging the old minister. He jumped a five-foot fence with the old pastor screaming for mercy. Three miles later the concerned crowd found them both sitting under a tree exhausted, but very much ALIVE!

Out with the Old and in with the New

Back in the good old days things were simple and appliances were easy to operate.

Mom had a wringer washing machine that really got our clothes clean and I loved the fresh scent of the bed sheets after being hung out in the open air on the clothes line all day.

But then in the late fifties my dad purchased a new one. I still remember us kids gathering around it as Mother made use of it for her first time. She put the soiled clothing in, pushing a button as we marveled in amazement when it filled up with hot water.

Father went outside to fetch an arm load of firewood but came running to the house when he heard Mother screaming. The fancy machine automatically started pumping out hot dirty water but the drain hose had slipped from the newly installed pipe shooting water all over the kitchen floor. Poor Mom panicked as she grabbed the hose trying desperately to fit it back in the narrow pipe. Father shot in the door, slipped and fell in the slippery water, landing on his butt and spraying his arm load of wood everywhere.

Mother was still screaming when she shoved the hose down the seat of Dad's pants hoping he could contain the discharged hot dirty water. He struggled to his feet looking like he gained fifty pounds on his rear end, then quickly unplugged the machine as steamy water rushed from his pant legs. Several months later a new item appeared on the market, a pop-up toaster. Again all us kids gathered around it glaring excitingly, waiting for the single slice of toast to pop up. This was great as Dad made the remark, "Wonder what they will think of next?" All of a sudden everyone was in the mood for toast, even sister Ruth who before never even liked bread. We must of went through one whole loaf of Mom's baked bread that first day.

Must have been about one year later when Aunt Goldie purchased a refrigerator. Everyone from up and down the road paid her a visit and marveled at the purring icebox. Mother nagged Father from that day on for one just like that, so finally he went to town take a look. Mother fell in love with a big white Frigidaire at the only furniture store in town. However, it was upstairs and the salesman said the delivery man wouldn't be beck until tomorrow, so with Mother's urging Father said he could carry it down the steep steps by himself, and haul it home. First he removed the door then fitted himself back first inside. I thought how much he probably resembled an ancient turtle as he adjusted the heavy load taking small steps toward the steep stairs. Mother started wringing her hands as her forehead wrinkled when Father's legs began to shake. He carefully made it down two steps alright but the back end of the frig caught on the first step. Seeing this I yelled, "Hold on Dad, I'll lift the back end up." He screamed, "No-o-o-o-o!"'

Too late. We all screamed as Father and the icebox made healthy bounces down the twenty-five steps. The salesman ran frantically to the front door in an attempt to open it but Dad and the frig beat him to it as wood and glass flew in every direction. He finally lit smack dab in the center of the busy street, surrounded by a bunch of busy bodies.

Dad climbed out unhurt, brushed himself off as the peeved salesman sternly pointed at the pulverized frig. Father pulled a comb from his back pocket, adjusted the part in his hair and said, "We changed our minds, she wants the tan one up there." The salesman went wild, told Dad to fork over the fifty dollars or he would swear out a warrant for his arrest. Dad lost his temper and poked the salesman in his eyes. Well, to make a long story short we became the owners of a scraped and dented frig but with a little work we made it purr to life.

Our whole family wondered if the light went off when the door was shut. Father tried in every way by sneaking up to the door and carefully shutting it. I volunteered to climb inside after removing the racks. I found the answer that day and everyone was very proud of me. Father said how brave I was and even promised to buy me a store bought Popsicle later that day. Mother rushed over to Aunt Goldie's house and proudly told her that Bud had made history proving the light does go out upon closing the door, and bragged that some day I might be a brain surgeon being so smart at the age of ten. Aunt Goldie stopped her short as she pointed to baby Shelly, explaining that he crawled over to the frig, pushed a button that the door normally would push and the light went off. She smiled big at Mother and said, "Can you imagine that, she's only three." I didn't get my store bought Popsicle that day but I still planned on being a brain surgeon!

8

Willie's Secret Weapon

Guess what Willie did in the apple orchard? It was a beautiful fall day down on the farm, we had a dozen apple trees in the orchard and following tradition we kids set out to borrow some from up the road. I was seven years old and Harry was eight as we packed two empty tote sacks in his bicycle parcel carrier. I sat on the crossbar, got fairly comfortable, then our ride began. We rode to the base of Gravel Hill, it was steep so we hopped off and walked to the top pushing the bike. The work was worth it though, as we sailed down the other side with the cool wind blowing in our face.

Old man Morris had several nice apple trees, they were loaded with big red delicious fruit. We stopped and studied the landscape, there were three barbed wire fences to cross but the tall grass would conceal us. Old man Morris had a big dog named Butch, so we checked the wind making sure he couldn't get our scent. It was a huge farm with big fields so as we studied the situation we decided to make our way to the forbidden fruit. We were up to the first fence when a noise drew our attention to their dirt road, there was Willie and cousin Freddy with their tote sacks. They dismounted their way towards us. We both said "darn" in unison, realizing Willie had control problems, especially during apple season—and most of the time ruined our secret missions.

Soon they were beside us as I pushed down on the rusted squeaking fence wire, then we passed through undetected.

On our elbows and knees we crawled to fence number two, passed on through, like warriors looking for a soldier with a full head of hair. Fence three was a snap as we looked at the drooping apples just waiting to be picked. We whispered a plan and soon our sacks took on fuel. After some time Harry whispered, "Look!" . . . I slapped the half-eaten apple from Willie's hand when I noticed two slimy cores down by his feet. This wasn't good. The fast movement caught old Butch's eye, as he let out a long howl and stormed towards us. Harry and I ran for the tall grass but Willie and Freddy climbed one of the apple trees.

I had foreseen this problem with Butch so I squeezed a small plastic bag of pepper from my pocket and sprinkled it near my feet. Butch's big nose was like a vacuum cleaner, his giant sneezes sounded almost human as he tore back to the house. Old man Morris flung open the porch door, leaped aboard the old Farmall tractor and steamed our way. We froze! All we could hear now was the idling engine as he stopped and walked around searching for us. Somehow I got a whiff of my own pepper, let out a sneeze as two huge hands picked Harry and me up by our suspenders.

Old man Morris was yelling at the top of his voice. I was terrified. Looking up, there was Willie in the tree straight above us. He was so terrified he fell from his perch, landing on old man Morris's shoulders. He let loose of Harry and me as he angrily groped at Willie, who now had a death grip on the old farmer's head. It looked like a wild horse bucking around trying to throw its rider. Now Harry and I yelled to Willie, "Bombs away! Bombs away!"

We heard a noise like someone tearing a rag apart. Yes sir, Willie let him have it! Old man Morris shook him off, let a few choice words fly that started with rotten, then raced to the creek on the other side of the orchard. We grabbed our tote sacks, which still held a few apples, then in minutes we were on our bikes. We let Willie ride far ahead of us, as Harry and I talked about another ruined secret mission. When we finally rode into the yard Mother yelled, "Where you boys been so long?" As I watched Willie pulling at the seat of is pants I replied, "We were testing out his secret weapon, and it really worked."

Today Willie is the manager of a large oil company in Ontario, Canada.

Get Rich Hunting Bottles

Bill and Dan were two happy go lucky guys back in the spring of '62. They would get up early every morning and go bottle and can hunting. Dan lived alone in a two-room house and had a dog named Lucky. How he got this name no one ever asked because Lucky only had two legs, one eye and his tail was some place else. Bill and Dan were friends but got real serious when it came to territorial rights while can hunting. Bill would take the left side of the highway and Dan the right, then vice versa.

One Friday morning Dan's side of the road wasn't producing too much. Realizing Bill had a toothache and wasn't anywhere around he crept over to the forbidden side and started picking. Dan figured he struck gold when he picked up an empty six pack of Pepsi bottles—but the gold struck back. Bill seemed to have appeared in thin air, calling Dan family names on his father's side. Then he swung a burlap bag half full of bottles, knocking Dan down in the ditch. Dan leaped up and pelted Bill with his bottle bag, as over twenty-four cans and bottles tore loose from their prison. Finally a husky resident pulled them apart, telling them to cool down.

Dan started telling the so-called intruder he was going to give the refundables to Bill anyway because he felt bad about his toothache. No one bought the good Samaritan story.

Bill also lived alone and had a cat named Happy. It received this name because her facial expressions always seemed to be smiling, exposing a rotten top tooth. Bill didn't care because he had two rotten bottom teeth. When he smiled it looked like someone left a gate open on a picket fence.

This one day Dan pulled into Bill's yard driving a tired beatup '48 pickup truck. He explained that they could get rich doing yard work, he even had a push mower and two rakes. They got a few customers, mostly uncles and aunts. Now Dan had a bad leg—happened when he was ten years old. He told Lester Davis, a new kid in town, that he was actually 'Superman' in plain clothes, tough as nails and he could fly faster than a plane. According to Mother, Lester took him serious, and pushed him off a twelve-foot fire escape, dislocating his right leg. So anyhow, this one hot day Dan and Bill were very busy, mowing, trimming and etc. After the long day they sat in the pickup counting their profits—they had earned sixteen dollars. Bill gave Dan six dollars and he pocketed ten. Dan asked him why he got more. Bill explained, "Because you only worked half as hard, your bad leg and all."

This went on for two weeks. Dan knew he was getting the short end but after all, he was making a living. Days later they got a job to paint a very nice house. The nice lady told them how to get there, which they did and prepared the house for paint. They leaned on an old wooden ladder against the house as Dan climbed to the eighth step, and the thing slipped. Bill screamed, "Oh, for the love of Mike." Dan sailed through the big window, spraying glass and blue paint all over the pretty living room. They were fired big time and now had a huge damage bill to pay. That night they decided to get out of the handy man business and start bottle hunting again, in order to pay the huge bill.

After six months of collecting bottles and cans they were out of the red. Then they got serious again and territorial problems arose once more. Early one morning Dan crossed the road and partook of Bill's cans, he caught him and grabbed a stick—forcing Dan to climb in a big steel water culvert to hide. Bill was ripping mad as he picked up a huge rock and smacked it down on the steel culvert. The echo was deafening as Dan rushed out holding onto his ears. Mother said to this day he still can't hear worth a can of beans! Dan rolled around on the ground, still holding onto his ears as Bill stole bottles from his sack. Seeing this, Dan sprang to his feet and the fight was on . . . Finally a local resident broke it up, and Bill and Dan certainly looked terrible.

Today Bill is president of 'Hall's Gingerale' in Salem and Dan is owner of 'Uncle Dan's Tonic' in Austin, Texas. At a recent reunion they hugged each other as Bill asked Dan, "Are you staying on your side of the road?" Dan cupped his ears and yelled, "What yaw say?" They both laughed and talked for several hours, all about hunting for bottles in the good old days.

Three Strikes, You're Out

We could tell something was wrong. The police didn't even knock on Aunt Hazel's door, they just kicked it down. She was our only doctor for miles around. We lived several miles from town on a country road that twenty-eight families shared. We totally depended on her for our medical needs. There were eight kids in our family and hardly a day passed that we didn't need her service.

Aunt Hazel was burly with broad shoulders and could lift her own weight, boasting three hundred pounds. Mother said this one night there was a dance at Sam Deming's barn. Hazel threw Uncle Ed, her husband of twenty years, a measured thirty-five feet on a bet from two rowdy farmers. However, when poor Uncle Ed got up to brush the straw from his trousers, she again grabbed him and broke her own record with a thirty-seven foot throw. This time poor Uncle Ed gathered up his lean one-hundred-and-fifteen-pound body and headed for home in the dim evening light.

The real trouble started on New Years night back in 1952. Wit White, an old man who modeled bathing suits, was struck down with an appendicitis attack. Aunt Hazel was called immediately and decided to operate right there and then, on the dirty, run-down dance hall floor. Wit was glad to see her, but had concerns about the baseball bat she was holding. All of a sudden she began to sing to him, "Take me out to the ball game, take me out to the game, there's one, two, three strikes you're out." Everyone drew quick gulps of air as she swung the bat, knocking Wit unconscious for his appendix operation.

People gathered around to help but when Aunt Hazel sliced off a patch of Charlie Reed's hair to test the sharpness of her knife, someone fainted. Dad said after she sliced Wit open she was confused to as to where his appendix was located, gave a tug on his heart then let loose just in time, realizing her mistake. At one time Wit started to wake up, then she again sang the baseball tune as everyone turned their heads and missed the crack of the bat and Wit went back to sleep. Miraculously, the operation seemed to be a success, but two weeks later infection set in and Hattie, Wit's wife, was a widow for the thirteenth time, being only forty-one years of age.

Aunt Hazel denied any wrong doing. The jury consisted of all relatives except one, a newcomer from Shag Harbour. My dad was Aunt Hazel's lawyer and Hattie, Wit's widow, hired a fellow from Halifax who bore the name Comitt Suicide. The judge, by the way, was Aunt Hazel's father, and when he introduced Hattie's lawyer's name it took three dozen gavel strikes to slow the laughter of the two hundred hillbillies who attended. Soon the trial got started as Aunt Hazel sat there chowing down a two-pound chicken that a jury member gave her. When the time came for her to take the stand, she refused until a tub of potato salad was finished that the judge gave her to snack on to settle her nerves. Finally she rose, pulled a chunk of chicken from her bottom teeth and boldly took the stand.

She told the folks she always sang to her patients, and when asked about her method of putting her patient out she replied, "I always use a soft baseball bat." The judge stood up with tears in his eyes, gave her a mighty hug and said, "Bless your little heart daughter."

Mr. Suicide blew his top, but didn't get the chance to finish his harsh criticism. The judge declared him out of order, as my two uncles threw him out in the street. The jury didn't even leave their seats, they just yelled, "She's innocent."

The trial was over, but Wit's widow didn't seem agitated, all she told the newspaper was, "Wit was a good husband. When I told him to take out a big life insurance policy, he did. Everything I asked him to do he never hesitated, one time he even ate glass. Now that ain't what caused him to push up daisies, ya understand."

Well, many years now have passed. I do miss Aunt Hazel and hold many fond memories, both gentle and brutal. I also sometimes hear the echo of us kids as we danced and sang around the old apple tree, "Take me out to the ball game, take me out to the game, there's one, two, three strikes you're out, when you get whacked from the bat by Aunt Hazel."

Gone Fishing

Back on the farm in 1955 things were going good. Townsfolk were happy most of the time, all they wanted was to be left alone. The town sheriff was a droopy old fellow who spent more time at the lake fishing than at the office. No one seemed to worry though, there wasn't no crime going on.

This one day some fellows came to town and slowly drove around, then after several hours they moseyed on into the sheriff's office. They seen a familiar sign, "Gone Fishing." They also noticed that the rifle and shotgun case was wide open. Later they learned it was left that way so folks could borrow them during hunting season. We soon learnt that these boys came from Halifax, part of the Canadian investigation team.

Two weeks later the old sheriff was put on unpaid leave as six red coats moved in to straighten up our disorganized town, as they put it. First thing they did was to stop poor old Ray Davis for speeding, yelling at him, claiming he was doing thirty-five miles an hour in a fifteen miles per hour zone. Ray argued back, stating his bicycle couldn't do thirty-five, his chain was held together by a nail, not only that, his pant leg was caught in the chain.

The following Saturday the air was filled with sirens. Seems there was a bad accident out by the county line. Charlie Reed was thrown fifty feet through the windshield of his old truck. He wasn't hurt too bad, but after the new policemen measured the distance he was thrown they wrote him a fat ticket for leaving the scene of an accident. That did it, everyone was mad, especially my Aunt Hazel. Her and Uncle Ed hopped in their car heading for town. She was going to give them a piece of her mind! After they entered the highway, the police stopped them, gave them a ticket for running on what they called "may pop tires." Aunt Hazel was so mad she bit her tongue; Ed tried to calm her down but to no good. She stood in a karate pose, and dropped the new policeman as though he was a toothpick. Finally he got back up, staggered around in circles like a leaf in a whirlpool, then took off running.

A town meeting was called that very evening. Boy, you talk about mad folks, the room was full of them. The next day their plan went into effect. My dad had a heavy load of firewood that needed to be unloaded. Aunt Hazel called the sheriff's office telling them that Dad had five gallons of moonshine hidden under three cords of wood. Within minutes the red coats ripped into our yard, jumped on the wagon and unloaded it with a great deal of labor. Finding nothing they gave Dad dirty looks as he waved good-bye and said, "Th-a-n-k Youuu."

Aunt Leafy reported to the police that her twenty-six-year-old daughter had left Ontario five months ago on a bus they called the "Bullet." She was to have arrived ages ago, but no sign of her. They launched a full-scale search, finding out the bus only had second gear. Finally, into town crept the smoking old bus. The police pulled up as Shirley stepped down. She was holding her stomach with pain. They asked her is she was O.K. Her reply was, "No, can't you see I'm about ready to have a child." The police started yelling, telling her she shouldn't have made such a trip being in the family way and all. Shirley glared back at them and said, "When I first got on I was only four months along, thanks to your dumb old bus."

Several months later our old sheriff was back and things again turned to normal, that is until Aunt Hazel got mad at her husband Edward, dunked him with honey, and ordered him to pick berries up on Yellow Jack Mountain. Dad raced to the sheriff to report this heartless act, but all he seen was the familiar sign, "Gone Fishing."

Harry and I Soaked Them

When we were kids living on a small farm there were many fond memories. Most of the time we played, but chores came on a regular basis and we knew the consequences if they weren't done. I remember this one day when some big shot from the government was coming to town to deliver a speech. This meant clean-up time, bath, clean clothes, haircut and clean fingernails. Oh how I hated such days!

The speech would take place at our schoolhouse auditorium, which held about two hundred people. It was a hot July afternoon when we piled into Dad's old car aheading to town. I was only ten at the time and had the option to stay home or go, I chose to go because we didn't often have a big get togethers, so I thought this might be exciting, and boy was I right!

The speech started, as the eighty-eight-year-old speaker started talking about the crops, cattle feed production and rising prices. The auditorium was packed and the heat had everyone waving paper fans trying to cool down from the July heat. The speech was drawn out, dry and boring. Most people in attendance was farmers and their families, so being the haying season, they were tired and sleepy.

Seated in front of us was a farmer nicknamed "Snake." He was bald headed and had beady eyes. Father said he got the nick name because his tongue was split. He went on to say that it happened in Ontario, where he performed in a circus act as a sword swallower. He accidentally burped when he was suppose to slurp, that's when the sword sliced his tongue.

It sure was funny watching the farmers trying to stay awake as their heads kept bobbing up and down. Then it happened. "Snake's" head fell forward with his tongue out, right on the neck of pretty Miss Pearl, who was high class big time. She screamed so loud that flowers flew from her rose garden hat. She turned around and slapped Snake on his bald head with all her might. It made a sound like a slamming car door. Miss Pearl's husband-to-be grabbed Snake, yelling at him that Pearl was spoken for. Poor Snake tried to explain that it was an accident but he wasn't believed as the bully yelled, "Look at ya, you speak with a forked tongue." While he was shaking his finger in Snake's face, he got bitten. Pearl was hysterical and started screaming for a doctor, thinking he might die from poison. However, it wasn't serious. After several minutes everyone settled down and again paper fans waved as the dry speech continued.

My friend Harry and I were very bored, so we asked Dad if we could go to the bathroom. He whispered O.K., but warned us to do so quietly. Once in the hallway we noticed the janitor's door was open. Curiosity got the best of us, so we tiptoed in to look around. There to our left was a big red wheel, attached to an eight-inch steel pipe. Harry dared me to turn it but I declined. He called me a scardy cat, so meaning no harm, I gave it a twist. We heard a terrible rumbling sound, followed by a bunch of horrified screams. Harry and I tore out of there in panic, as the overhead sprinklers in the auditorium let loose. People were yelling, pushing one another around as they scrambled for the exits. Everyone looked like they fell overboard as the janitor rushed into the closet and shut off the water.

My Aunt Hazel's makeup was running down her face, she reminded me of Bozo the clown. She put the janitor in a headlock, while yelling at him about his sick jokes, as the karate chop made his legs buckle big time. Harry and I started crying, telling Dad we didn't mean to. It took three farmers to free the thankful janitor, as Aunt Hazel glared now at us. She started rolling up her sleeves, to us this only meant one thing, RUN.

Well sir, Harry and I had to spend two weeks mopping the auditorium. No damage was done to the building, but we had no desire to sit down on the job while performing our duties, I'll tell you that!

A while back I got a letter from my friend Harry, and in it he said, "Hey Bud, remember the day we made it rain on that hot July afternoon?" I wrote him back and said, "Sure do, every single time I pass a schoolhouse."

9

River Man Tom Pickering

Thirty years ago when I first met Tom he ran the fish rearing pond on the Trask River. One day he invited my brother Jake and I to a salmon dinner at what we called Uncle Tom's Cabin. We drove twenty miles from town that day but when we arrived at Tom's we retrieved a rare sight. Old Tom came bursting out the door with a frying pan held high in the air chasing a big otter, which was running for dear life with the salmon we were to have for dinner. Both the otter and Tom disappeared over the hill towards the River. We could hear Tom yelling, "Stop, stop," but maybe the otter didn't understand English because he disobeyed Tom's orders as he hit the water and was gone.

Tom was spitting mad when returning and asked us if we liked hot dogs. We started investigating the crime scene and soon we seen how this slick salmon poacher stole our dinner. Tom had left the fish in his sink while he went outside to fetch a big cast-iron frying pan. When returning to the kitchen he caught the uninvited guest on a chair, which he had pushed over to the sink, snatched the bright salmon and shot past the screaming host.

Anyway, the hot dogs were good and soon Tom calmed down after mopping up the muddy otter tracks. The next week Tom again invited us for dinner, promising venison. So we again drove the twenty miles and upon arriving out shot

Tom again through the open door chasing a deer with a broom. Apparently Tom had left the door open as a nervous buck walked in, tempted by his house plants. My brother looked at me and said, "Looks like hot dogs again."

One other day Tom invited us and ten others to his cabin for a horseshoe pitching party. It was a pleasant day and everyone was having fun until a friend of Tom's showed up, she was known as Passionate Possie. No one could figure out how she ever received that name and as you read on you might wonder too. Possie wanted to pitch horseshoes but after losing six to twenty-one she went wild. Tom tried to calm her down only to have a big flower pot smashed over his head. My little brother told her she shouldn't have done that to poor Tom, but instead of an answer he was whisked off his feet, landing in the fish pond with two thousand Coho salmon smolts.

If I had known she was a martial arts expert, I probably would have remained standing but I didn't. She dropped us like bowling pins during a strike. My little brother drug himself from the pond soaking wet, when he spotted us rolling around on the lawn in pain he shook his fist at Passionate Possie. Wrong thing to do. Jake took off running like a stone from a sling shot with Possie in hot pursuit. Mother said they ran for two miles but Jake was saved when a good Samaritan slowed down enough for him to hop in the car. Mother also said his clothes were even dry from the wind and friction while running for what he thought was his very life.

There was this other day when Tom had purchased a new rifle, 300 mag. He called and asked us to come up and sight the canyon cannon in using some paper bull's-eyes. We asked him several times if he was alone up there and questioned the whereabouts of Passionate Possie, he promised she wasn't there and hadn't seen her for several weeks. We took turns shooting the new rifle when Tom handed me some hot reloads he had made. This one shell didn't look right and I had trouble getting it to chamber. But what I didn't know was that Tom overloaded the shell by mistake. I aimed the thing and pulled the trigger, fire and flames shot from the muzzle, the barrel flew off as the stock split into three pieces. We never did find my glasses and our ears hurt for weeks.

Tom's cat jumped on the dog's back and took off running, looking like some crazy circus act. The three of us staggered all over the place, kneeling every once in awhile, holding our ears. Tom was yelling but not being able to read lips his words were useless. Tom has long since retired and has moved closer to town. I will always cherish the good times my brother and I had up there in the good old days, or were they?

The Big Ball Game

The big ball game was to be played Saturday afternoon in the cow pasture. I was Babe Ruth, Freddie was Ted Williams and Harry was Mickey Mantle. In 1955 we did our best with what we had, two rubber balls that were badly dog-bitten with chunks taken out and cut off boat oars for bats. My glove was ripped with the thumb missing, our bases were real classics, dried cow patties. Kids showed up from town, up the road, down the road and across the river. Our audience consisted of parents, grandparents, farmers and two old tramps we didn't know.

We tossed the bat to pick our teams. I chose Harry right off the bat because he could hit the ball a long way. With nine kids on each team, Willie threw me what he said was a curve ball, but it hit me so I took first base. Harry came up to bat as the crowd was sitting on hay bales cheered. Willie tried to act like a big shot as he waved Billy toward the pitching mound. Billy was the catcher, and Willy the pitcher. He put his glove over his mouth so we couldn't read his lips to steal a sign. But the thing was, we weren't using signs. Finally he pitched and Harry belted a home run, so now we had to search the blackberry bushes to find the ball, and ten minutes later we retrieved it as the game once again started, two to zero.

Willie wound up to pitch, Ray held his bat high but the ball went low because it had rolled in fresh cow manure. Ray swung, fouling the ball back smacking poor Dad between the eyes, turning his face rosy red to a light shade of brown. He whipped out his hanky, wiped his face, assuring the folks he was OK. Ray ended up striking out as Willie boasted about his fast ball.

We had to stop the game again because Molly the milk cow just had to show up and of all the places to bed down, she picked second base. The crowd booed but Molly didn't care, she just lay there chewing her cud and swatting flies with her tail. Finally Father coaxed her away with fresh hay as the game resumed.

Freddy stepped up to the plate making believe he was Ted Williams, grabbed a hand full of dirt, spit on the ground as Willie threw a pitch in there for a strike. Freddy got mad and said he wasn't ready! However, the next pitch he hit a single but tried to make it to second base where he was tagged out. We had to stop again, this time Bert, the Jersey bull, just has to stroll into the ball park, stop at first base, donate another steaming base, then walk off like he did a big thing.

Our side finally got out so we sat at two to zero. A small kid named Frank hit a line drive. Harry dropped the ball from his mitt, then from nowheres Rascal, our dog, seized the soggy ball and ran into the barn. A ruckus broke out as Frank crossed the home plate, claiming a run. We started screaming, "No fair, no fair," but it counted anyway. We couldn't retrieve that ball so we used the second one, and the only one. Lawrence stepped up to the plate with two strikes, but with the third pitch he smacked a homer so deep we didn't even bother to look for it.

We decided to call the game a tie, everyone started to leave when the two tramps waved us over where they sat with dark glasses on and long gray coats. What happened next put us on cloud nine. The taller man stretched out his hand with a bright white new baseball signed Mickey Mantle. The second man did the same with the signature on the ball being Ted Williams. They said that's who they were as our eyes grew bigger than the baseballs. When the two men walked away we went crazy, jumped around and yelled our thanks behind them. We sat on the hay bales just staring at the balls, then we raced towards Father telling him the good news, but he didn't act surprised. No one believed us then and no one believes us now. Father said they were just two berry pickers, but we know the difference, huh Harry!

What Was That Santa Said?

The snow was white and pure, even the fluttering flakes brought joy to us kids as our tongues stuck out to catch a few of the wayward ones. All we wanted to do was get our first taste of Christmas snow. It was only three days before Christmas Eve so everyone on the small farms around the tiny town of Shelburne, N.S., was beaming with excitement.

The year was 1952, there was ten inches of snow on the ground when my dad hitched up Old Dime the plow horse to a big wooden sled called a go-devil. I grabbed the ax as we piled on along with Rascal, our beloved dog, and four of my sisters. Then off we went to cut a tree for our living room at home. We traveled a good distance into the north woods.

The big fir trees were modeling their new uniforms of icy white, as a white-tail-deer waltzed across the frozen pond. Dad finally spotted a Christmas tree that looked just right, so after our approval, his ax bit in as us kids started a snow ball fight. The tree was loaded along with us kids as we filled the wilderness of the north woods with Christmas carols.

The jingling jingle bells gave us a time to reminisce about Dad's stories of the good old days and the past traditions such as this one. It was a wonderful experience. Soon it was time for the skating party down at the lake. I still remember my uncles and aunts and us kids on that Christmas Eve getting ready the food, skates and lanterns. Then at dark many sleds being pulled by horses arrived along with a huge full moon shining on the fun-packed celebration.

Homemade ice cream was a must, so my cousin Harry and I were put in charge chopping the ice for the six hand-cranked ice cream makers. This made us feel like big shots. Everyone was skating and singing as the full moon scattered its light waves to give the ice a sparkling complexion. Right in the center were four picnic tables loaded with goodies that folks had baked, boiled and fried.

Pretty soon I saw Mother's big fuzzy mittens go into motion. That waving meant only one thing, it was time for cousin Harry and me to cut the ice. To this day I wish we had of been obedient and went to the frog pond to perform our ice chopping chore, but instead we disappeared from the lighted circle of lanterns to the outer part of the lake. Soon the ax was employed and in no time at all we all had good ice but left a huge hole in its place. It was just like I told Harry, no one in their right mind would be skating out this far, and even if they did what chance would it be to fall through the hole we just cut. Harry, who was very wise for his eight years on earth, agreed. So we loaded our precious cargo on our toboggan and headed towards the lighted figures skating in the distance. When we arrived once again Mom's big fuzzy mittens went into motion, as she patted us on the back in recognition of our quick return.

What a wonderful time everyone was having. They were singing aloud, skating hand to hand while the giant oak trees on shore were showing off their muscular shadows as the moon shown behind them in their decor. Laughter danced all around, only taking second fiddle to the high strung "Turkey in the straw" tune played by Uncle Nick on his homemade violin. Yes sir, memories were being made that would last a lifetime.

I was puzzled to the whereabouts of Father, since he had left some time ago. Us kids still believed in Santa Claus and had no idea that Father himself was the jolly old fellow. He had skated to the other side of the lake dressed in his Santa suit, as he peered through the darkness waiting for his arrival signal. Everyone went quiet, then we heard from far off, "Ho, ho, ho, ho." Wow, you talk about excitement, my heart hammered. Cousin Billy started crying, and Harry started shaking, I myself was so excited I forgot to breathe. He was getting closer. In the moonlight we could see his bulky figure. Goose bumps ran up and down our backs, then the "Ho, ho, ho," could be heard even louder. This was the real Santa, yes sir, right here on our lake, excitement ran wild.

Then terror struck. Harry nudged me. I looked at him and his eyes were scary looking. I thought how much he resembled a hoot owl in a herd of mice. Then I felt warm water run down my pants leg when he said, "The hole we cut!" Oh, no, Santa was heading right for it. I tried to scream, my mouth didn't work. I looked at Harry again for wisdom, he smelled awful and looked frozen, and then it happened. Everyone exploded, grabbed several lanterns and skated hard to the thrashing Santa. Mom grabbed my hand, as her screaming was dreadful, tears streamed from my eyes as she towed me along. Uncle Bob got ahold of Santa, as the others grabbed at his bloated red suit. He looked funny splashing around there. Then I noticed he had a bald spot on his head, just like Father's, his long johns were the same too, and even his voice. The yelling sounded the same, but whatever he was screaming about, I couldn't hear. Mom's big fuzzy mittens were firmly plopped over my ears.

That Cat in the Volkswagon

We moved from Canada in 1959 to the U.S. Things were much more advanced than what we wished but we did our best with what we knew and had. After moving into a nice house in Weymouth, Massachusetts, we started to lose most of our hillbilly habits and this reminds me of what happened in the mid '60s. Father ran an ad in the local paper for someone to do yard work around the place. After several replies he was called many names when the caller asked about wages. Dad thought he was being very generous with his one-dollar-an-hour pay rate.

One day he received a call and the guy seemed more than happy to take on the job, made arrangements to meet us at our place around 5-ish. Father was sitting on the front steps and an old Volkswagon bus pulled into the yard—with flowers painted all over it. Dad walked over to greet a long-haired man with small round glasses.

The man wound down the window and asked Father if he was the cat who ran the ad. Father questioned his eyesight and told him he wasn't a cat, but did run the ad. Later he told Mother that he got a whiff of some weird smelling smoke that poured from the flower wagon, as he called it. They talked for some time, Dad never seen a hippie before so he made remarks about his long hair and other things he didn't understand. They walked around the yard seeing what needed to be done. Now at this time dad smoked cigarettes, but when he drew out his pack it was empty. The hippie seen the situation and gladly offered Dad one of his. Father said he never seen such a funny looking cigerette before as he lit the thing up. Minutes later we heard Dad laughing and patting the hippie on the back. When Dad finally came inside he just sat down starring at the black and white TV. Mother glared at him and said, "You're gassed!" Father just burst out laughing.

Now Father was very hungry as he walked out to the kitchen, rubbed his chin, then stated he couldn't remember what he was looking for—then again started laughing. Mother later made the remark that he was always very forgetful and even when he was a kid his parents would let him hide his own Easter eggs. Soon it was bed time as we all turned in. The hippie slept in his wagon, as Mother turned out the lights. Father always wore white long johns to bed, and around midnight he felt sick so he went outside for fresh air. His bright whites glared in the darkness.

He walked over to the Volkswagon bus and peeked in the window, making sure the hippie was alright. He started throwing up, making ghostly heaving sounds. The hippie sat up like a half-opened jackknife, looked out the window and screamed loud enough to wake the entire house. The old bus was rocking and rolling as the hippie kept shouting something about a big "Caspar." He finally fired up the engine and disappeared in a blanket of smoke. Us kids, along with Mother, rushed outside asking Dad what had happened. Father wasn't feeling good, so while still holding his head he said, "That long-haired fellow has a memory worse than mine. I must have told him my name a dozen times, now he rips out of here thinking I'm someone named Caspar!!"

Mother helped Dad back inside—put a cold towel to his head, then remarked, "You poor thing, better get back to bed—you're as white as a ghost. . . ."

10

Cloud Nine

It was a warm summer day back on the farm. A giant blue sky with puffy white clouds lay back as though they were taking a Sunday afternoon snooze. I was seven years old at the time and loved every day in the country. We worked hard but the rewards outnumbered the chores. One day I was laying in the hay field looking up at the clouds, two big white ones looked like a bear chasing a cow, then as I chewed on a long stringy straw I heard a truck coming up the road. This caused excitement because living six miles on a dirt road in 1952, only five or six would be seen in a given day, and they would be neighbors most likely.

I ran to the road to see who was visiting. The strangers were driving a new 1952 Ford pickup and towing a large trailer. They stopped and asked me if my Dad was home. I pointed to where he was digging a well so they drove to that spot. They shook hands with Father and before long I saw Dad nod his head as the two men opened up the back trailer door. I ran to the scene to satisfy my curiosity and there in the back was huge basket and a lot of tanks and a huge canvas. Dad spoke first, "What in the tarnation is that?" They said it was a passenger balloon, and they wanted to set the thing up in our hay field.

Soon uncles and aunts showed up along with my friend Harry. The two men busied themselves unloading the material and then helium was used to make the huge canvas rise.

What a sight! Father was very excited and started acting like he owned the thing, yelling at the neighbors to stay back, etc. Soon the two men were ready for a flight test and asked Father to join them but he declined, telling them that he had an earache, but Mother told the neighbors that he was terrified of heights.

Up, up they went—everyone was cheering and chattering loudly as Father acted like he was one of the crew. Soon they were back, tossed down the ropes as we tugged on them until the basket plopped to the earth. We hitched it to the heavy sand bags as neighbors shook their hands thinking they were famous.

The two city slickers asked Father if he would guard the craft for a couple of hours while they went to town for a bite to eat. Father was delighted and gladly accepted their three American dollars. Dad yelled at Harry and me to get away every time we got near the thing, even chewed poor Uncle Bob out when he touched the basket. Finally everyone left except Father. Harry and I went for a swim and when we returned we noticed Father had climbed in the balloon and fell asleep. Mother would say he could fall asleep anywheres, she just wished it wasn't always in church. Ever since I was two years old I remember Dad always talking about cloud nine, how he would love to be there everytime he got mad about something. It was always cloud nine this and cloud nine that . . . so this gave me an idea. Harry and I played some hardy tricks on Dad but now we could make up for them. We snuck up to the balloon, could hear Father snoring, and untied the ropes from the heavy sand bags. Up, up went the balloon, up, up, went Dad. Harry and I slapped hands hoping the craft would deliver him to cloud nine where he would be overjoyed. He was about one hundred feet high when he awoke, looked down and let out a scream, then started yelling for help. Farmers and families came running but couldn't help in any way. Mother dropped to her knees in prayer. Father was jumping up and down, terrified and screaming things like we had never heard him say before. In a few minutes he disappeared from view and neighbors cried in horror telling Mom he was a good man. Uncle Nic was sobbing badly as he told Mom that space aliens would get him. Uncle Bill made the remark that he deserved to go, but not this way, as Mom and us kids all cried in unison.

The balloon and my dad drifted towards Birtchtown Mountain, which was occupied by hillbillies. They weren't seen much, once or twice a year when they came to town for supplies. All we learnt that day was that they shot the balloon down thinking it was from outer space. Father was shaken up badly but was OK.

We didn't know nothing about this as we all cried and hugged each other. Harry and I tried to explain all we wanted to do was to put Dad on cloud nine. Mother was horrified and we were too when she screamed, "There ain't no cloud nine!" Now Harry and I cried along with everyone else, tears and nose blowing was so loud we didn't hear the pickup roll in. The two men arrived with Dad sitting on the back. Suddenly I looked up and saw Father rolling up his sleeves. I yelled at sobbing Harry. We sprang to our feet and took off running. Mother tried to hold Father back, trying to explain to him about our intention but he ripped away in hot pursuit. Now the crying ceased for Dad and started for poor Harry and me. He finally caught us and I will never forget his gruff voice when he said, "I'll show you two clowns cloud nine!"

Willie Did His Job

It was a cold crisp day with six inches of snow on the ground, but to us kids the day was beautiful. There was gleaming white snow with a bright blue sky, a priceless picture. The year was 1955 in Nova Scotia, Canada. We lived on a dirt road several miles from town, a big family of ten in an old farmhouse we dearly called home.

In the spring and summer we walked to school but in winter Mr. Gilbert Perry would pick us up in his 1949 Ford, a four door. On our road there were twelve kids who needed the services of Mr. Perry. We always dreaded the lappers, that's what we called them, because not having room in the car us older kids would be seated first, then the younger ones would sit on our laps. This isn't a fond memory of mine at all. On this one particular day, I remember every event just like it was yesterday and as you read on you will understand why.

My cousin Harry and I had a friendly snowball fight on the side of the road as we waited for our ride to school. Soon three of my sisters arrived from the warm house along with Harry's only sister, Diane. We could hear Mr. Perry's car coming from the clicking of the tire chains, this meant the fun was over and we were on our way to school.

It felt good to get inside the warm car. The girls always got to sit in front, that was the rule. Us guys didn't like it but respected the decision. Harry poked me in the arm and reminded me that it was my turn to hold Willie on my lap. I got a sick feeling in my stomach as the tire chains whacked the fenders in a steady rhythm. Now Willie was a round fat young kid with a million freckles. We liked him a lot but he had a problem. He lived on an apple farm and Mother would always say that his control problem was his Mom's fault. She would can the apples too early, giving them a physic condition. Willie of course, who loved apples, was a receiving victim.

Soon the car started filling up. When we neared Willie's house, I crossed my fingers, hoping that he was sick or something, but then I saw his rabbit fur cap. I opened the door and said, "Morning Will." He jumped on my lap, as Harry giggled, while pinching his nose, then with his other hand, he pointed to Willie. I saw no humor whatever in this remark.

There were three hills on our road, Gravel Hill, Torri Hill and Thrill Hill. If a car could reach 50 miles per hour while crossing Thrill Hill, one would get a thrilling feeling in the pit of the stomach. This was caused by the car leaving the ground a couple of inches. Today we wanted to be thrilled until we heard Wille's stomach growl, that's when we spoke in unison and asked Willie if he was OK. He assured us he was, so now only a half a mile away from Thrill Hill we all yelled loudly, "Gill, Gill, give us a thrill, Gill, Gill, give us a thrill!" Gill was a nice old man, he looked exactly like the captain on Gilligan's Island, even the cap was the same. He leaned forward, tromped the gas pedal to the floor; the old Ford trembled as the engine roared, trying to produce the horsepower that us kids and Gill demanded.

Excitement rose to an exploding level, the interior of the Ford shook violently as us kids bounced up and down in great vigor. Gill had a death grip on the steering wheel, as our teeth clicked together in tune with the slapping tire chains. The noise was terrible. Now I felt the vehicle raise, we will lifted from our seats, the only thing I could see now was the rear end of Willie at eye level. Then I heard a noise like a dog growl. It happened. Willie had a big accident. When the car landed I reached for the window but it was frozen. We screamed at Gill to stop, he hit the brakes sending the car into a fifty-foot skid sideways. We piled out as though the car was on fire. I took gulps of fresh cold air once outside. Even though I still had some of Willie with me, we walked to school as Gill took Willie back home to change.

The teacher asked us where Willie was. We told her that he had some unfinished business to do. I'll never forget that day even though it was almost fifty years ago. Today Willie is the president of a big oil company on Ontario, Canada. He is married and has a son named Willie Jr. His son spends a lot of time in the big backyard among a dozen or so apple trees.

In the Beginning

Over the years I have made several appearances as a guest speaker at clubs and luncheons, and the most often question I am asked, such as the last one in November at the Shiloh Inn in Tillamook, is just how many of my stories that are published are true. My answer is always the same, "Most are, and the others are close to it." The people's names are real as I remember them as a kid growing up in Nova Scotia, Canada.

Harry was my best friend, he and I shared the same school, fields and back woods. My uncles and aunts I mention are real, even Aunt Hazel. I will often exaggerate them, such as describe them bigger or smaller than they really were, adding some spice to explicate them or vice versa. All my writings are based on true stories that have impressed me in my younger days up until now.

I also wish to thank all of you who read my stories. I love the letters you send, the phone calls and the many people I meet who mention how similar their growing up in the good old days were, but end their conversations with "although my memories aren't quite as colorful as yours." Well now, having said all this, have I ever told you the story about how I ended up in Oregon? Well, here goes.

Times were hard for my dad to make a living back in 1959. We sold the farm with several acres, a big lake almost in our backyard, a big house with ten rooms, a cellar, the house fully furnished for three thousand Canadian dollars.

We set off on a foggy morning in a 1954 four-door Ford, after a bunch of tears and hugs from our dear neighbors and friends we were on our way to Weymouth, Massachusetts. There were eight of us kids plus Mom and Dad, fresh from the sticks, heading to the United States, which we had heard many stories about but had never seen.

At Yarmouth, Nova Scotia, we boarded a ferry along with the Ford, and crossed the Bay of Fundy, which took six hours to cross into Bar Harbor, Maine. After leaving the ship we were detained at the border, but after presenting our proper papers, vehicle check and many questions we were once again on the road with a head sticking out of every window. Poor Dad, he had never been on a four-lane highway before and trouble started immediately. He was poking along in the left lane as horns started blowing all around us. Thinking the folks were kind and giving us a welcome, we all waved and exchanged a friendly smile for grim facial expressions and a shaking fist. My dad thought they knew my Aunt Hazel back home, she was a boxer and well known in the province of Nova Scotia. So he would smile and shake his fist back in tribute of recognition. This went on for several hours, until flashing lights pulled in behind us. Dad kept going, winked at Mother and said, "Look Daisy, what a friendly bunch, they're even snapping pretty lights behind us, I'm glad now we decided to come to the States, ain't you?" Mom didn't get a chance to answer. A loud speaker rang out, "Pull to the side, right now."

As Dad pulled to the shoulder and stopped he made the comment that if Aunt Hazel was here right now, he would give her a big smooch. We were impressed with the state trooper's shiny uniform as he asked Dad to step out. He bluntly asked Dad if he was a wise guy. My dad answered, "Yeah, you can say that, ain't much I don't know." The trooper's face reddened. He slapped a yellow piece of paper at Father and yelled, "Here's a ticket for traveling in the left lane." Dad hugged the fellow and said, "Ain't you kind, I don't mind traveling in the left lane, I'll stay in it all the way to Massachusetts." Something wasn't right, we could tell that by the harsh words and the red face of the trooper. After he left, Dad got back in, looked at us with a hurt expression and said, "You can't judge a book by its cover," then we started out again, this time in the far right lane.

Next day we arrived at our destination, Uncle George and Aunt Jenny's place. They lived in the large town of Weymouth. We weren't comfortable because of the small house, small yard, but some how we adjusted to our surroundings.

Now folks, don't miss my next story. I'll tell you about starting school in the city. Dad gets hit by a bus walking across the road on a don't walk signal. It will be titled "Hicks from the Sticks," a true story.

My Mom, Daisy

My mom is a very special person. She brought eight of us kids into the world even though times have been hard. She can tell stories of the good old days and now at the age of ninety her memory still serves her well.

When we were kids she was our mom, our nurse, teacher, problem solver and most of all a good wife to my dad. I remember as a teenager coming home late. Mother would listen for the turning of the key, get out of bed, making sure I was alright. One night like always, she awoke again, came downstairs to make sure that I made it home safely. I got mad and said a mean thing, Mom just hugged me as I felt a warm tear fall on my arm, and to this day I cherish her soft words, "Son, when you grow up to manhood and get out on your own, I'll still worry each night but you won't know it 'cause my tears and fears for your safety you won't see, I'll just hold them here within 'cause maybe you won't need them anymore."

Well, I grew up alright, but I still need my mom, there is just something in a mother that keeps you on track, and when problems arise that you can't solve, Mother is always there with the answer. My mom's hips are weak now, my sisters say that's because she packed me around till I was four years old. I considered myself smart, why walk when you can get from point A to point B higher and faster when you're being packed by your mom.

I remember back ten years ago when Mother was a young eighty, she went to Washington state, to my sister's house. Joyce and her husband Ron was taking a three-day trip and Mom was to clean and house sit for them until they returned.

Mother had never seen a garage door opener before, so she didn't pay much attention to that little button until the back door locked behind her. Well she thought, no problem, the garage door was wide open and there stood freedom. Before leaving the garage she just had to push that door bell button, down came the garage door. Poor Mom, she drug her feet around and around that garage looking for an opening, but none could be found. Realizing she was trapped, she prepared for her three-day garage stay. After discovering a box of apples, she knew food was there along with cold and hot running water. A further search revealed plenty of cleaning stuff. There was Mr. Clean, Pinesol, Pledge and for the garage windows, good old Windex.

Day one she washed all the walls and floor, day two, the windows were so clean a bird flew into them thinking the glass was gone. Day three she did all the wash and scrubbed the washing machine and dryer so hard, the seven-year-old machines looked like Sears had just delivered them. Around five-ish Joyce and Ron arrived, they didn't notice Mother glaring out the garage window as they made their way inside the house. Realizing everything looked the same, panic set in thinking the worst. Ron raced to the garage door and as it rose there stood Mother with cleaning rags in hand and wearing a smile. The whole family sure got a big laugh out of that and eventually so did Mom.

Then came the day when her new microwave was delivered, never had she seen such a contraption. I was working in the backyard when she raised the kitchen window, asking me if I would join her in a big bowl of baked beans. Of course I told her, then she smiled and said, "I'll put them in my new microwave son, it will get hot a lot faster, she smiled as she nodded. Suddenly I heard a muffled backfire from within the kitchen. I raced in the house to find what made the sound when I heard "B-u-u-d, help!" What a sight, she was covered with beans. It looked as though she suddenly busted out with thousands of age spots, the kitchen was a shade of bean color as pieces of tin foil dangled from her white hair. I have never seen such a sight in my life, beans were on the walls, even her cat Herb left a bean trail from the window sill to clear under the sofa. We kids got together and cleaned her house until it was bean free. She never again used tin foil, matter a fact, I don't think she ever used her microwave again either. I love my mom, and when she has her senior moments all I can say is God love her, for she is my dear mother.

11

The Corn Family

When we were very small children in Canada we looked forward every night before bedtime for my dad to tell us a story. Our favorite story was "Jack in the Beanstalk." My dad had a way of telling stories that would make you think you were right there and it was happening right in front of you. It seems Dad's back in the good old days spent more time with their kids, and story time was very important to us all, it kept us a very close-knit family.

I remember a story my dad told me many years ago. I was probably only five or six years old, but I remember it as though it was yesterday. He told of a fellow named "Kan Corn." He took a wife, her maiden name was Sweet Davis, but now married, her name became Sweet Corn.

Mr. Kan Corn was a kernel in the military, but came home every chance he got on leave. They were happily married and lived on a small farm in Shelburne, Nova Scotia, Canada. Everyone said they came from good stalk. After his duty was up in the military he came home to stay. Two years later they had a son, whom they named Cob. He had long ears and silky hair. Besides bringing great joy to his parents, he was a happy baby, big rosy cheeks and hardly ever cried at night. He grew fast, it was the fastest thing that he ever did. Then at nine months old he muttered his first words. Mr. Corn picked up little Cob over his head, the baby was delighted and along with a cute little laugh came the words "Pop, pop."

Two years later they had another son whom they named Chuck Corn. He was husky and loved to eat. At the age of twenty-two he opened a factory where they produced breakfast cereals that were mostly of the flake varieties. The factory soon received the name "Corn's Flakes Breakfast Foods." Cob, his brother, was part owner, and they became well known for their products all over southeast Canada.

Chuck Corn soon married a little gal, her name was Indy Ann, now being his wife she became Indy Ann Corn. They too bore a husky baby boy who practically ate them out of house and home, and at three months of age he was too big for the crib that the Corn family had passed down for generations.

In the late 1940s trouble struck the well-managed factory. Some thugs got hold of the Corn's Whiskey and raised the dickens inside their plant after midnight. Cob, however, was working late in the office. Hearing the commotion he stepped out to find the disturbance. The thieves jumped him and being out numbered he really got creamed. Chuck Corn got word of the trouble and hopped in his pickup and rushed to his brother's aide. After driving to the factory he opened the door. Unfortunately Chuck Corn got popped a good one, but managed somehow to make it to the "can" and locked himself inside until the police arrived.

Things finally got back in order and a trial was held a month later. Folks were ready to string up the thieves, but the law discouraged this, promising that a speedy trial would be held and the ones responsible would be prosecuted to the full extent of Canadian law.

The province Court House was packed on that hot August morning. After the crooks' attorney told the jury that the Corns didn't have a foot to stand on, things went wild.

The Corns broke out in a tussle, and a free for all took place. One of the Corns got a bite taken from his ear, and luckily only two of the Corns got popped. Soon order was contained and the Corns were rewarded a big field of money. The thugs were all sentenced to five years in the "Can." The following week the local newspaper devoted the whole front page to the Corn's trial. They ended the story by stating that the whole thing was a very corny case.

How to Get a Job at the Fire Department

In the early '60s I tried to get a job after school to save money to buy a car someday. Being only fifteen years old no one was eager to employ me so I flipped through the papers for work ads. It didn't take long before I came across just what the doctor ordered, someone to sell fire extinguishers door to door. Father drove me to the address and I wasn't impressed because the whole back side of the factory was burned out, and when I pushed the door bell sparks flew everywhere. I spit on my shirt sleeves to discourage the sparks, just when a man opened the door. He was sloppy looking, big pizza stains on his white shirt, the knees were missing from his trousers and his cowboy boots were so worn out I could see Kelloggs Cornflake box tops pushing through the sides acting as soles that were badly decayed. He could only get two words out at a time then he would yawn. I could see a piece of bacon, or some kind of meat swinging from his back molars as his tongue would lash out trying to free it during his yawning spell. His eye brows were bushy and shot straight up pointing to the ceiling, reminding me of Uncle Lew's old '49 Hudson windshield wipers on his old car back home. I seen enough, so I walked back towards Dad's car to go home, but he told me to get back in there to take the job, he couldn't afford to feed me forever, then he took off in a cloud of dust.

Finally I signed some papers and was handed a box of small fire extinguishers. Sloppy Sam, that's what they called him, told me he would pick me up and demonstrate the product to the householder, after which I would be out on my own.

Next morning I greeted him on time. He had a milk ring around his mouth, then all of a sudden he leaped from the car and heaved all over our nice cat, Raymond. He kept making dry heave noises, so while he was busy trying to get well, I glanced around his car. What a mess. He had a pipe wrench for a steering wheel, the interior smelled like the town dump. After awhile he slowly got back in, looked at me with big watery eyes, and told me he felt much better. He went on to say that he had eaten rotten eggs because his brother had made a fifty-cent bet that he wouldn't.

Finally we backed out of the driveway, but I felt sorry for Raymond our cat, he kept running into trees head first, apparently temporarily blinded from Sloppy Sam's regurgitated breakfast. After a short drive we stopped at a house as Sloppy Sam handed me an extinguisher. He also packed one as we stepped up to the door.

A woman now stood there as Sam told her how wonderful our product was and politely asked if we could step in and demonstrate how quickly a grease fire could be put out with our "Little Marvel Fire extinguisher." She hesitated but agreed as Sam poured bacon grease in her kitchen sink, then he lit it on fire.

The blaze was two feet high. The poor woman put both hands on her cheeks. Sam yelled out, "Have no fear, Sloppy Sam is Here." He pulled the pin but nothing happened, the woman struck a high-pitched screaming spell. Sam grabbed my "Little Mavel," but it didn't work either. The flames now lapped at the kitchen curtains. Sam had an accident, I saw the back of his pants move and he smelled awful. The woman's daughter appeared and she also started screaming. Poor Sam, he started to make loud moose calling sounds as he desperately splashed water on the out-of-control fire.

The curtains burst into flames and Sloppy Sam burst for the door, jumped in his car and left the scene with screaming tires. The fire trucks roared in, neighbors came running to watch the excitement.

Finally the fire was out. The police questioned me all about what had happened, and seconds later they caught Sloppy Sam. They had a court trial. Sam didn't mean no harm so all he got was fifty hours of community service and that was at the town's fire station.

Believe It or Not

Thirty years ago, Tom Pickering, Burt and Tony went to Ukiah on a deer hunt in Eastern Oregon. The day before they left Tillamook the three hunters excitedly loaded the Jeep and hitched up the fifteen-foot camping trailer. They gathered at Tom's place to hear stories of huge bucks told and retold.

Old Tom, a senior deer hunter, told many tales of the early days but Burt and Tony always said that Tom liked to water down the true facts but they didn't mind because his stories were very colorful. He told of a huge mule deer that stole his rifle one year. He shot the trophy mulie, which was such a wide rack that he placed his rifle in the deer antlers. Then he pulled out a camera, stepped back to snap a picture, but the deer arose and darted off with the rifle in its rack.

Old Tom tore out after the deer with great vigor. The mulie was running straight towards a camp where a bunch of hunters were gathered around the cozy campfire. Now old Tom was trailing a ways back but heard the excitement from the surprised campers. One yelled out, "Look at this fellows, a big buck packing a rifle." When Tom stumbled in view all scratched up and bleeding he yelled at the wide-eyed hunters, "Get out of the way boys, I want to give this old buck a sporting chance." Then both he and the buck disappeared in the trees, this of course is according to Tom.

After a dozen more stories everyone hit the hay. The alarm clock was set as everyone prepared for morning. At five A.M. the coffee was abrewing and minutes later they were on their merry way.

After eight hours of driving up popped a sign, "Ukiah—thirty five miles." They turned off the highway, then stopped to check their gear and get a bite to eat. Before starting out old Tom decided to ride in the tired trailer that they were pulling. Burt wanted to join him so Tony slid under the steering wheel and away they went.

Approaching a small town called "Pilot Rock," something dreadful happened. Tony put the Jeep in low gear because they were descending a steep hill. He heard a loud-pop, then said to himself, "Oh my goodness, some poor soul just lost their trailer," as it whizzed by at twice his speed. Old Tom screamed at Burt, "It's an earthquake." The noise was deafening as the trailer tongue dug in the pavement and sparks flew everywhere. Old Tom didn't think the trailer was moving, so he opened the door and stepped out. Burt froze and rode it out and finally the thing came to rest in a campsite, as though someone parked it there.

Old Tom was taken to the Pendleton Hospital but released the same day with two broken ribs. Burt was so shaken up that he asked for his mother, but next day he made the remark that he was totally joking. After the tow truck was called and a new hitch welded on they finally got to their camping spot and next morning went hunting. Poor old Tom, he was hurting with his broken ribs and had to sit on a stump every few feet.

Then about ten o'clock a big buck wandered out in front of him, he up and fired, down went the deer. Tom limped over to where it lay, but his broken ribs forced him to sit, so he straddled the deer to rest. Then all of a sudden the animal rose, apparently Tom only knocked it out. The wild ride was on. Tom slammed his rifle in the antlers as he held on for dear life, they tore through the trees at neck breaking speed, then a clearing came into view. Off to the left with mouths wide open stood Burt and Tony in disbelief. As old Tom bounced up and down on the deer's back and sped by his two astonished buddies he yelled, "I'm taking this one to camp boys, meet me there, then I'll fetch you another."

Even to this day old Tom says, "This is my story, and I'm sticking to it."

Where in the World Is Garibaldi?

Enos was a fellow who liked a lot of privacy. In 1964 his daughter got very sick, so the doctor recommended that she go to Portland to see a specialist. Enos thought the world of his daughter Polyann, so when she ran out of options for transportation, Enos, who hardly ever left Garibaldi, agreed to drive her there.

He was a young man of eighty-eight years old, his daughter was twenty-two, and his tired old Ford was a 1945. He would pull up to a gas station, tell the attendant to fill the oil and check the gas.

The Wednesday they left it was raining cats and dogs. Poor Enos took a wrong turn, and was lost in and around Tillamook most of the morning. Then around noon he finally found Highway Six, and soon they were eastbound at last. At the sixteen-mile marker Enos fell asleep at the wheel. It was a miracle, because when he awoke, Polyann had fainted. It was then that he realized that they had driven almost a mile on the wrong side of the road. He wheeled her back on track with a bunch of mad sounding horns. Finally Polyann came to, and told Enos about a chip truck that came barreling down at them, but said the driver was defensive, and he swerved just in time to miss them. Enos looked at his daughter with wide eyes and said, "Oh good heavens, I'm sure glad I wasn't awake to see that."

When they were approaching the summit Enos pulled his machine in second gear. Later Polyann said when they finally got to the top, she counted twenty-six cars and twelve trucks lined up in back of them, some stalled out because of dead batteries caused by excessive horn blowing. It was dark when they got to Portland. Realizing they had missed their appointment they spent the night in the first motel they came to.

Next morning they tried to find the medical building on Lovejoy Street. Enos spotted a building where a man came out carrying a dog with a bandaged foot. Thinking this was the place, he and Polyann parked and went inside. Enos walked up to a guy in a white suit, then asked him if he were a doctor. The gentleman replied, "No, I'm a veterinarian." Enos then coughed back, "I don't care what your religion is, I'm looking for a doctor." Enos, not being well educated, came back out with a red face and some humble directions. Finally they found the medical center and Polyann was rushed into surgery to be operated on for gall stones. Enos was devastated when they told him she would be there for two or three days. He wanted to go home and so did Polyann. Enos was right there by her side after the operation as she begged Enos to take her home. Enos questioned the doctor, but no dice. So he whispered to Polyann that when the lights go out, so would they.

The woman sharing the room was having a face-lift. Enos never saw her, but overheard the nurse kidding around with her friend stating that she would make King Kong look cute. The nurse gave both women a sleeping pill and ordered Enos out along with the lights. Enos waited an hour, and crept back in the room to fetch Polyann. Not realizing the nurse had switched beds around, Enos made his play. He pulled the bed sheet up over Polyann's face, and quietly wheeled her to the exit door. Little did he know it was the face-lift gal. Things went well until Enos tried to set her in the car. She awoke and stared at him, he stared at her, then the screaming started. It sounded like two police whistles as they took turns screaming.

Enos tried to speak but all he could managed was "Pol, Pol, Pol." Then his screams made the whole street light up. Soon after cop in the city it seemed was bouncing Billy clubs off Enos's bald head. Then they tossed him in the wagon as he kept yelling, "What did ya do to Polyann's face?" over and over. Next day things got straightened out. Polyann somehow got Enos out of jail, but before he left the sergeant, thought he would have a little fun with Enos in front of the guys. He asked, "You say you come from Garibaldi. What planet is that on?" Then they all laughed. Enos had the ability to turn both eyes blood red ever since he was a kid. The sergeant's eyes grew wide, then even wider when Enos squeaked, "Jupiter, Jupiter, Jupiter."

Hicks from the Sticks?

It was a very stressful time moving from Canada to the U.S., but after many emotional trials we settled into a half-balanced life style. I started a new school in Weymouth, Massachusetts, and the very first day I got myself in a fine mess.

The dress code was sports coats and slacks. Now where I come from sports coats meant an old jacket you took to a ball game, and slacks, well, that was what mother called us kids when we sat around not doing our chores. That first morning I was so proud all dressed up in new Levi's along with my new hickory shirt, it was simply superb.

As I walked up the long sidewalk kids started laughing. They would whisper to each other what I was in for. Half way to the front door I knew something wasn't right, this one teacher glared at me then snapped out the words I'll never forget, "Smart aleck aren't you?" Being polite I answered, "Oh no ma'am, you got the wrong fella, my name's Bud Cunningham." She grabbed me by the shirt collar and said, "Young man you march yourself right down the hallway to the principal's office now!" Mom always taught us to obey our teachers so I cuffed my heals together, saluted her as I planked my feet down, performing a march, as she had requested. The rest is too awful to mention.

It was a quiet ride home in the janitor's old car. I had only five minutes to redress while his old junker car made sounds from the jungle. Mom was really upset as she tossed clothing from an old suitcase. She found a suit coat that was grandfather's. When she gave it a shake, moth balls bounced off the floor all around us. The thing was four sizes too big and had a big mustard stain on the left collar where Grandfather had dropped a hot dog back home at a ball game. The pants she tossed me once belonged to Elliot Ness, so she said, as she sent a safety pin in where a button once was. When I came downstairs I felt awful. My Uncle George looked at me and said, "You can't go to school looking like that, look in the mirror there, you look like a big bumble bee." Mother started crying.

I hated to leave the house but finally got in the stinking old rattletrap as the janitor kept staring at me, then he kept muttering, "Oh, oh, oh, oh." When we got back to school I

119

was sent home again but this time I walked. Next day was better. Mom got me clothes that fit the dress code, so I seated myself in Mrs. Moss's classroom. She was a stuck-up well-educated city slicker who looked down at her nose at me. All of a sudden she said, "Bud, do you think you know how to spell river." I thought for a moment then said, "Mrs. Moss, do you think you know how to spell river?" She got insulted, huffed up, and spoke, "Ha, I don't think, I know." I threw my hands in the air and said, "Don' feel bad Mrs. Moss, I don't think I know either." It was another short day for me, but I enjoyed the peaceful walk home.

Next few weeks went better until the teacher tapped her pointer and said, Class, next week we're going to learn some Italian language, do either of your parents know how to speak it?" I raised my hand because one day I heard Dad tell Mother he knew some Italian. The teacher didn't like me and she made it very clear when she got up in my face with her teeth gripped, "Hey chubby, you'd better not be fibbing." Anyhow, she gave me a note to take home inviting my Dad to school to give the class a lesson. Father agreed to go and that day Mrs. Moss bought ice cream and cake, tied balloons

and ribbons all around and boy was I proud. Around two o'clock right on schedule came my dad, as the class cheered and clapped. I felt so good, especially when Dad bowed. The teacher looked at him as though he might have been a professor at one time. She then said, "I hear you know a little Italian." My dad rubbed his chin, and proudly muttered, "Yeah I do, he works at the gas station on Second Street."

Well, another short day for me, but I loved the father and son talk and the walk back home.

12

Like Father, Like Sons

Russell McCoy was the meanest kid in school. He lived way back in the woods with his mom, dad and three younger brothers. He only came to school when he felt like it, which was about two days a week.

One freezing December morning he climbed up on the schoolhouse roof, stuffed an old burlap bag down the chimney where on the other end sat an old wood stove which kept us twenty-one kids warm. Smoke poured from the furnace as the teacher herded us outside for fresh air. When the janitor, who was Mr. Barkhouse, went up after him, Russell slipped the dirty charred bag over his head turning his face black.

Mother said when he was a baby his mother would sit him in the corner and feed him with a sling shot from a distance of thirty feet. He grew up and married a woman named Berr. They had eight kids of their own, all boys, but the sad part was they followed in Russell's footsteps, and very seldom went to school. Somehow they all got common jobs, but not having discipline they disobeyed most rules.

One day Russell took his oldest son to work with him, he wanted to show him how to snow the boss. However, he seen through the scheme and fired Russell from the potato fields. He turned to the boss and brazenly yelled, "I was looking for a job when I found this one Bubba." A few days later

Russell got another job in a fish factory in Barrington. He was doing alright until a well-dressed young man walked in one day looking for the boss. The guy talked to the owner for a half hour, pointed to some blueprints he drew, then left with a handshake. At lunchtime Russell asked the boss who the young man was. He told him it was his son, that he was a graduate of Yarmouth University and made big money as an architect.

Then the boss asked Russell what his sons did for a living. Russell rubbed his stubble chin, cleared his dry throat and said, "Billy works at the hospital, he's a financial whiz, he helps folks who are broke, get back on their feet." However, Russell failed to tell him that he put crutches together for a living. Then Russell spoke about his son Knute, told the boss this story, "Knute works in Halifax at an eye clinic, he helps people see better. Why, the first day there, he went from the bottom to the top in that seven-story building, just like that." Then he clicked his fingers. But what he failed to say, was that Knute worked there alright, but he washed windows so folks could see better, and as for going to the top, it was the elevator that he used. After that he told him about Percy, his oldest son. He made the remark that he traveled a lot in his job. Claimed that just last week he took a big trip down under, but come to find out Percy tripped on the cellar steps and fell all the way down, finally ending up under the basement stairs.

Russell no more had made these statements, when Percy showed up. He bluntly held out his hand and asked his dad for a dollar. That's when Russell's boss jumped up and spoke. He asked the guy his name, and when he said Percy the boss got suspicious and asked him a question pertaining to Australia. "Say, what is it like down under mate?" Percy looked confused. Russell, started trembling, then Percy looked down at his scraped up legs, thinking he must have heard about his fall, and said, "Oh, it's dark and dirty, and lots and lots of cobwebs." After saying this Russell quickly handed him a dollar and pushed him out the door. The boss piped up and said, "Ha, I never thought Australia was anything like that." Then Russell said, "Oh yeah, the boy wouldn't lie, I taught him not to."

The Smart Rat Versus the Dirty Rat

It was a real dry year back in 1955, the ground was hard and the crops on our small farm were feeling the pinch. My dad made the remark that he had to sit on a bag of fertilizer to raise an umbrella. Being the middle of September this wasn't good, winter was approaching with only a few crops to put in storage.

I was ten years old, there were six kids at the time plus my dad and mom. To add more misery, the rats were moving in. My dad sat traps and lowered the population, but one old rat he couldn't catch. We caught sight of him maybe five or six times, after which we gave him the name "Tex." This was due to the fur on his head, which looked like a miniature cowboy hat.

One morning we went to the trap that was set in the closet, and couldn't believe what we saw. Old Tex rustled up a clothes pin, pushed it under the tongue of the trap, then gorged himself with rank cheese that served as bait. Dad grew furious as Mother started yelling in the kitchen. Old Tex had eaten a hole in her newly baked bread; there was no toast for us that morning. After several more unsuccessful trapping events Uncle Bob let us borrow his rat killing cat. When he put the cat on the floor he winked and sounded off with the remark, "If old Capone here doesn't catch that tricky rat in two days, you can throw me in the lake."

Now Uncle Bob must have had all kinds of confidence in his cat to make such a remark. It was a well-known fact that he only took a bath once a month, and that isn't counting wintertime because he always said, "That water is just too dang cold."

That very night around twelve o'clock, the entire house came back to life, something awful was happening in the kitchen. Dad raced downstairs in his gleaming white long johns. When he yanked open the kitchen door, he had to leap high in the air. Capone, the tomcat, ripped on by, and riding on his back was Tex the rat, his teeth clamped down on the cat's ear. Dad opened the back door looking for a club. He gripped onto an ax handle. Out flew the two. Dad swung the handle and made contact. Poor old Capone, Dad said some kind words as we engaged our shovels.

When we went back to the house, guess who was lapping in the butter dish. Poor Mom, she didn't care about the butter, it was the dish handed down by her great-grandmother. Dad curled his fingers around the broom handle and let fly, missed the rat but the dish wasn't so lucky. Next morning as we got out of bed we heard Father scream. His big toe and the one next to it took a direct hit as the rat trap clamped down with a whack. Apparently old Tex pushed the trap right where Father's foot had landed every morning. Later that day Father purchased some rat poison; three chickens lay dead the next day.

Dad now got a twelve-gauge shotgun and waited for old Tex to come out of the rhubarb patch. We heard the shot, so we dashed to the scene. When we got there Dad's cap lay on the ground. Buttons from his shirt and the shotgun lay there in two pieces. Dad's face was black from gun powder, as he yelled, "that miserable rat, that miserable rat." After close inspection it was plain to see old Tex had stuffed food for the winter in the shotgun barrel, causing the overused gun to explode when fired.

Somehow we made it through the winter with a lot of prayer and the old smoke house. Poor Dad, he took a lot of static from everyone who heard about Tex, so he made the comment that the word rat would no longer be permissible around him. Two months later Dad settled down, even his nightmares came to a halt. He once again was a great Dad to us kids, that is until Uncle Bob paid a visit.

We were sipping lemonade on the porch. Uncle Bob approached softly, removed his brown derby hat, brushed off the lint, then said to my dad, "Where's my cat Capone?" My dad said, "He's in kitty cat land." Uncle Bob, who had never went to school said, "How do I get there?" Dad started laughing, then us kids torched off. Uncle Bob backed up until he was in the hay field, cupped his hands over his mouth and yelled, "Grant, you're a dirty rat." Dad was a fast runner for a large man and once again Uncle Bob took another bath.

Do Drop In

Harsh words were said, but no one really meant anything by them. We had a big farmhouse with eight kids in Canada, the year was 1951 on a hot July day. My dad was very irritable mostly because of the heat and really laid into Grampa for getting the old Farmall tractor stuck. One word led to another as both men started screaming things that us kids shouldn't have heard. Grampa threw a roasted chicken that splattered all over my dad, Father grew so angry he poured a dipper of hot gravy down Gramp's coveralls causing him to invent a new dance.

Mom stepped in only to have a hot biscuit bounce off her forehead. It was a bit frightened but couldn't help joining in the free for all. I grabbed a hot potato and heaved it with all my might, even though it blindsided my dad, he somehow knew it was me. I started to run as he reached for a kindling stick. The chase took us outside as I prayed for my feet not to fail me now. I started to zigzag and because my dad was a heavy man his pace slowed down as mine sped up. Behind us was a string of folks, all family except an insurance man who was working the farm area. He joined in the feud thinking it was a game we all played.

Finally when my dad tired and sat on the wagon the poor salesman made a sales pitch to him. My dad flattened him as I watched the wind toss his papers around the field. The old salesman started flopping around on the ground like a fish out of water. Mother and Gramma got him on his feet and while helping him to the house promised to mend the seat of his britches, which was badly ripped out.

Later that day Dad and Grampa still were yelling, then Dad told Grampa to get out of the house and not let the door hit him in the rear while doing so. Grampa was devastated, hurt big time. They had no place to go as Gramma took hold of his suspenders, laid her ancient head on Gramp's chest and cried as though her heart had broken. Mother tried to reverse Dad's remark but Grampa, being sensitive and proud, looked up at Dad and said, "We'll start packing."

Mother got on Dad big time. She told him to apologize but Father had his pride also and just couldn't do it. It didn't take the poor souls long to pack, only one suit case was needed for them both as us kids pulled on their hands begging them not to leave.

We got the hugs from them like always as they arm to arm started their walk to town, turning away my uncle's offer to take them there as we cried. We thought we were watching Grampa's curly white head and his half-hitch limp for the last time. Needless to say it was a sad time but we were reassured of seeing them again when Dad said, "They will be back before sunset."

Well, sunset came but no sign of our beloved grandparents. That night Dad loaded the car and we set off to find them. The wrinkles made waves on Dad's worried forehead. No sign of them anywhere but while we were searching, the twosome had returned unnoticed.

In the house upstairs there was a spare room that we never used because it hadn't been finished, just joist beams with no floor, which happened to be directly over the dining room. They had moved in there and they were as quiet as mice and somehow spent the night and the next day there.

Dad spent all that day looking for them as Mom set the table like usual, still placing dinner settings at the grandfolks' place hoping for their safe return. My dad came home at dark, hung his hat, didn't say a word as he quietly disappeared in the bedroom. The house was without voices, the laughter wasn't there, the only sound we heard was the mournful crying by our dad. The insurance man was invited to dinner, Dad's way of apologizing for his actions, as we gathered once again around the table for a meal. No one felt like talking but soon my dad looked at the salesman and said, "You know, if Grandpa and Gramma could suddenly be seated here for supper I'd give you this here contemplative pocket gold watch, yeah, I surely would."

Just at that time Grampa lost his footing, stepped down on the false ceiling and came flying down through the Sheetrock as pieces flew everywhere. Grampa landed practically in his chair unhurt. You talk about rejoicing! Dad was so happy that he hugged Grampa; he almost broke as the squeaky voice of Gramma sounded from above.

Things started back to normal once again, that is until the salesman held open his hand, expecting the gold watch.

Tony Got His Clock Cleaned

Antcy was an old man who lived by himself and was thought to be the cleanest man in Nova Scotia, Canada. His house was magnificently clean and Father made the remark that he took four baths in the lake one August day. I was ten years old and my friend Harry was twelve. One day we decided to climb the mountain to visit Antcy. We asked Dad if it was OK and he agreed but told us to mind our manners because Antcy was a hermit and wasn't especially fond of people. Dad went on to tell us that Antcy was so clean that sometimes he would squeak while walking, and not only that, he also was the strongest man that lived in Nova Scotia by far.

Antcy lived up on Strawberry Mountain where he built a log cabin but all the furniture and appliances he bought in town and packed them up the steep mountain trail on his back. Father said one day he stopped to see Antcy while up there hunting and noticed that he had a brand new wood stove. Father asked him how in the blue moon he got the four-hundred-pound thing up the mountain? Antcy said, "I packed it on my back, weren't too hard, the only thing that gave me a little trouble was the fifty-pound bag of potatoes in the oven, they kept trying to get out."

We asked Dad more questions about Antcy so we pulled our chairs closer as Father went on. He stated that Antcy once had a wife but it got too much for her as he kept cleaning every chance he got. She would wash the dishes then Antcy would redo them. He would scrub the floors sometimes twice a day. Father said his dog had a very shinny rear end, Antcy had scrubbed all the hair off the poor thing. He was going to throw water out the window one day thinking it was open, actually the glass was so clean it looked that way, the water splashed back to him but his wife didn't. Father said one day two trappers paid a visit on the mountain and gave Antcy some static and he ended up cleaning their clocks for them.

We thanked Dad for the details as we made ready for the steep climb. Just before leaving we remembered Dad's remarks of how clean Antcy was, so we tried to look neat. Then we remembered Tony, he lived down the road and everyone knew him as an inelegant wise guy that no one could stand being around, we also remembered that he had a grandfather clock that didn't work, the hands were stopped on three. Father would often remark that the clock was right twice a day. That was more than anyone could say about Tony. He took the clock to Halifax and was told it needed cleaning, but once he heard the price he slapped the owner's face and told him his gears were also stuck. I remember Father saying, "I don't know how he ever made it to be thirty-two years old."

Anyway, we stopped by Tony's and told him that Antcy could clean his clock, all he had to do was to give him some lip, according to Dad. Tony smiled big thinking that won't be hard. We loaded the old clock on his old wheelbarrow as we started our climb. Tony kept yelling at us to push harder but our pace slowed even more. When we stopped to rest Harry whispered to me, "Why are we helping him?" Before I could answer Tony grabbed us, started calling us names and even gave us a number of how many bones he would break if we didn't push on the wheelbarrow harder.

Finally we arrived at Antcy's place. He came outside the house and glarred at us. I couldn't help thinking how much he resembled Mr. Clean. He told us to scat and we weren't welcome there. I told him I was Grant's boy and explained that Tony had a clock that needed cleaning as I swung around pointing at the wheelbarrow. His gruff voice pierced our ears as he roared; "Don't clean clocks!"

It was now I remembered Dad's words, if you give him any lip he will clean your clock. So I urged Tony to get started and boy he did. We only heard two thumps, one when he hit Tony and the other when Tony's butt hit the ground. We started crying as we loaded Tony in the wheelbarrow, leaving the wounded clock for the second trip. Tony was out cold as we hustled him down the trail. We made it to Harry's house as his dad loaded Tony in the pickup truck and tore off towards the hospital. There were a lot of people in the emergency room but the only one that shed a tear was his mother. After an hour Tony came around and his eyes finally focused on the doctor. His first words were, "Did I get my clock cleaned?" The doctor nodded and said, "Yeah boy!"

13

Talk about Cheap!

When I was growing up on a small farm there were two men I will never forget. They were identical twins and at the age of thirty-three they moved to our small town. Aunt Hazel was the first to think that maybe they weren't on the level and she made it well known. There was no way to tell them apart, both wore the same kind and color of clothing, even their voices were the same. Aunt Hazel said they should be run out of town before they commit a crime.

One was named Mike and the other bore the name Ike. One day Mike went to the barber shop for a hair-cut. When the barber was finished he turned around to put the two bits in the cash register. Ike snuck in and sat in the chair with a full head of hair. When the barber turned around Father said that his eye balls hit his eye glasses, knocked them to the floor. He thought he lost his mind as he muttered, "Wh-how-wh-who-di-." Anyhow, Ike got a free haircut and Ward the barber spent the evening in the Jolly-HoHo Tavern until closing time. Father made the remark that both of them was so cheap it was pitiful. He went on to say though that they were the ones that invented copper wire; they got into a tug of war fight with a penny.

Father also stated the reasons their noses were so big was because air was free. Mother tried to cover my ears with two pot holders and scolded Father severely concerning his rumors.

One hot August day both Mike and Ike set up a Kool-Aid stand in the center of town. Mother said that three cents a cup was outrageous but managed to scrape up six cents from her worn-out purse for Harry and myself. One taste and we both spit the Kool-Aid out, and after numerous complaints the cops discovered that they were using only one package of Kool-Aid to three gallons of water. The whole town went into an uproar, and Aunt Hazel was fanning the flames. She plainly wasn't thinking when she told Uncle Ed to throw a rope over a tree limb, suggesting a hanging. When it came to buying food they didn't. Even though they had a lot of money they spent very little. Both were tall and skinny and earned the nickname, the two-step boys. Father said they got that name because being so thin they had to take two steps before their pant legs would move.

One day a hot apple pie disappeared while cooling on Aunt Hazel's windowsill, right away she blamed Mike and Ike. That very evening the cops found the two pie burglars down by the bridge, throwing up big time, and lying next to them sat Aunt Hazel's half-eaten apple pie. When the cops contacted my aunt and told her how sick they were she dropped all charges and denied the fact that her pie was ever stolen, not wanting people to think of her as a lousy cook.

It was also a known fact that Mike and Ike were very lazy. Father said when they went fishing they would get mad when he hooked a fish. He said one day they were lying back to back in the shade when a new shiny sports car passed by. Ike told Mike about it and all he said was, "Sure wish I was facing that way!" Aunt Hazel said the fastest thing that they ever did was grow!

Mike and Ike finally bought a small farm, and because Mr. Durkee was broke and needed back surgery they got the place for one third the price. Aunt Hazel said the joke was on them because there was no well and the only water had to be packed from the creek for a half mile up hill. After a few weeks Mike surprised the entire town with an old treasure map, which he swore was authentic. He claimed this was the reason he bought the farm because in the backyard Blackbeard himself buried a treasure chest and according to the map it was about forty-five feet deep.

Able bodied men from town and farms offered to dig for a share of the wealth, which Mike and Ike agreed to. Aunt Hazel told the neighbors now she thought they were on the level after studying the map. She commented that they were good men after all, and she would supply the food for the diggers and in turn she would get a share of the wealth too. Mike and Ike eagerly agreed. After ten days of digging and reaching past the forty-five-foot level, water rushed into the hole causing everyone to scramble. Mike and Ike acted disappointed, saying that the map must have been unreliable and all the fifty-foot hole was good for now was a well.

Aunt Hazel blew her top and started chewing Mike and Ike out right up in their faces. She smacked Mike over the noggin with a shovel and heaved Ike down the well. Dad and Uncle Ed lowered a rope and retrieved him as Uncle Harry rushed Mike to the doctor's with a cracked head. Mike and Ike filed a lawsuit making everyone involved pay them twenty-five dollars each. Mom said that Aunt Hazel was so mad that her bobby pins vibrated out of her hair. As they filed from the courthouse Aunt Hazel got up in Mike and Ike's face again yelling, "The only pirates that ever set foot on that farm you bought is you two."

My Dad and the Bear

When we were growing up in the wilds of Canada there seemed to be a lot of bear trouble around the small farms.

They would stuff themselves on apples and anything else eatable, which made them a pest. Dad and my Uncle Ed were going to shoot the bruin on this one day, or so they thought. Both awoke early one bright morning, grabbed the beat-up rifle and away they crept in the woods.

Dad at on a stump and sent Uncle Ed ahead to flush out the troublemaker. Three hours passed without any action, so Dad lay back and before long fell asleep.

My friend Harry and I wanted to get in on the hunt so we trailed behind the two at a distance. We heard a terrible commotion up ahead, it was plain to us that Uncle Ed had run into the bear, or the bear had run into him. Harry and I ran into the clearing to see Father fast asleep. The screaming got louder and with a tremendous crash out of the woods popped Uncle Ed and behind him was the bear. He was yelling at Dad to shoot, but just waking up to such a horrible situation, the gun flew left as Father went right.

The bear forced Uncle Ed up a tree. Dad climbed a huge spruce and so did Harry and I fifty yards away. The bear growled with anger as he stood up swatting at the tree limb where Uncle Ed was standing. Getting tired with him, the brut made a visit to Father's tree, ripping off chunks of bark, forcing Dad to climb even higher. Next he paid Harry and me a call. He stood up on his hind legs. I looked down noticing that his left eye was filmed over and most of his big yellow teeth were broken off. We remained in the tree trembling with terror.

Dad yelled at me to throw bark down at him to keep his attention while he quietly descended the spruce tree. We threw bark down making the bear really vicious as his growls actually hurt our ears. Dad hit the ground and managed to reach the old rifle. He yelled at the bear and when the bruin swung around Dad fired. The bear fell flat on all fours and made no movements as Uncle Ed, Harry and myself descended to the ground. I will never forget what happened next and neither will Dad.

Father always carried a backpack with many handy items including a Kodak box camera. He handed it to Uncle Ed and told him to snap a picture of him sitting on the bear's back. What's wrong with this picture?

Apparently Dad only grazed the bear's head, knocking it out. When he jumped on its back the bear sprang to life and took off running with Dad holding on for dear life. His screams blended in with the bear's, making a dreadful sound. Uncle Ed threw me the camera as he picked up the rifle and started running in the direction taken by Dad and the bear. I couldn't believe my eyes, Father actually rode a wild black bear. No one would ever believe it! Uncle Ed finally found Dad laying by a stream dipping cold water on his cuts and bruises. Knowing the bear could sense injury, we helped Dad to his feet. We kept looking over our shoulders as we hustled him out of there and an hour later arrived home. Mother was horrified as she kept repeating, "I knew it, I just knew it."

Well, sir, the story hit the papers about Dad's bear ride; no one believed us or him. It was just like Aunt Hazel said, "No one had ever ridden a bear and no one ever will." Dad couldn't sleep well. Mother said he would make bear sounds when he did sleep and even scratch on the bedroom walls. One day he tackled Grampa in the hay field making growling noises. He even bit him on the chin, sending Grampa into a panic as he screamed, "Bad bear, bad bear."

When he returned to normal Mother sent for the doctor, who stated that Father was suffering form bearaphobia, no doubt brought on by his horrible experience. One night he attacked again. Uncle Nic went outside to check on his chickens when Dad grabbed him from behind sounding off with deep bear growls. His panicked screams made Uncle Ed's dogs howl almost one mile away. Then Father gave him a bear hug which Mother said made Dad turn him loose because Uncle Nic an hour earlier had eaten a big pot of cowboy beans forcing him to backfire. Father's eyes even watered as he stumbled backwards searching for fresh air.

Aunt Hazel later said, "Serves Grant right, I don't think Nic should have been so rude but like I always say, any port will do in a storm."

That was the last time Father thought he was a bear and a few weeks later Uncle Ed remembered snapping a picture just as the bear arose with Dad on its back that day in the woods. They rushed the film in for development and sure enough, Dad was on the bear's back.

Many years have passed since that day, but the last time I went to a rodeo the announcer said, "Next up is the bareback riders." That's when I remembered my dad back in the good old days, or were they?

The Barber Shop

When we were growing up in Canada one of the things we dreaded the most was getting our hair cut. Our country barber was none other than our Aunt Hazel. The only other one that cut hair was Ol' Bill, better known as the scalper. It was Saturday afternoon also my birthday, so with a quarter in hand I slowly started my walk to Aunt Hazel's house.

I remembered how rough she was, so this slowed my pace as a youth of eight years. I knocked on the door. When she appeared, I couldn't forget how huge she was. Then she yelled, "Get seated boy, I aint got all day." Her small kitchen was sky blue and like always there was cabbage boiling on the old wooden stove. Then from out of nowhere a big horse fly dropped in. Aunt Hazel, being a very clean and tidy lady, grabbed a kitchen towel making slaps at the thing, even though my haircut was only half done. As they both gathered around me I put both hands over my head trying to avoid being an anvil to dispatch a dirty old horse fly. The insect made some unusual flight attacks, as Aunt Hazel started going wild. All she cared about now was to do away with this fly any way she could. I felt panic taking me over as her huge muscles rippled with every swing of the towel. Then she hit the pot handle with the boiling cabbage as hot water flew everywhere. Poor Aunt Hazel got burned pretty good all over her wide hands. My dad drove her to the doctor and was told that she wouldn't be able to cut hair for a long time. Boy did I get laughed at in school, with my half a haircut.

That following week cousin Harry and I decided to take over for her, but the complete lack of customers was irritating. We practiced on the farm animals first. Old Rat, our dog, stayed under the doorstep for two days, just itching real bad from his close shave.

Next Saturday my four uncles could be heard singing and telling stories down by the lake. Mother said for us kids to keep clear of them, because they were making moonshine. Anyway, we grabbed our scissors and crawled closer to our jolly uncles. It was plain to see that the whole four of them could use a good hair cut. We realized that every Saturday they would take a catnap, so we clicked our scissors and waited in the tall grass.

By five o'clock the singing stopped, they were soon snoring loudly, so we snuck closer to our customers. Both Harry and I thought that they would be real grateful, getting a free haircut and all. I started clipping away on Uncle Bob first, everytime I started to even one side of his beard the other side needed more trimming, soon all that was left, much to my surprise, was a small patch of hair underneath his chin. Somehow I also ruined his black curly hair, leaving him with a wobbly mohawk. It was now that I heard Harry crying. Oh dear Lord, he made Uncle Ed's head look like a spotted leopard. He started backing up, crying with a runny nose, yelling over and over, "Look at poor Uncle Ed, look at poor Uncle Ed."

Maybe we shouldn't have done it, but we put the scissors in Uncle Lew's hands, then we took off running. A few days later Uncle Ed and Uncle Bob finally got nerve enough to show their faces and their bad hairdos. Oh, by the way, so did Uncle Lew, along with his big black eye.

Is That a Skunk or a Cat?

It was a hot August day, temperatures at noon had reached 102 degrees. Wherever there was shade that's where you would find people in and around our small town. Father made the remark about our vegetable garden, stating that another three or four days of this and our garden would be gone. Even us kids were cranky but got active towards evening, as it cooled down in the 70s.

Eight of us kids were sitting on the porch—the year was 1958—watching the fire flies and the full moon. Sister Joyce came running up the steps and somehow my foot tripped her causing her to fall down, skinning up her knees. She started bawling as Mother took her to the bedroom. I too started bawling as Father took me to the woodshed. I was ripping mad, I didn't deserve the woodshed all the time. My sisters lived like queens and were treated with dignity.

Sunday was gone by Monday was just as hot. The well was dry so we had to pack water from the lake to the house, a good quarter of a mile. This one day when we arrived with our buckets of water Mother made the remark that some kind of animal had slipped through the open cellar door and ordered Dad to go in after it. Father was a brave man but questioned Mother pretty good about its size and teeth. She said it looked a lot like a house cat, and after thinking about it she was sure that was what it was. This made Father feel brave as he grabbed the fishing net and started his descent down the dark cellar steps. I had also seen the intruder and I know a skunk when I see one, but decided to remain silent.

The cellar door had a big wooden lock on the outside. Father yelled at me—making sure I held the door open wide because after netting the cat he would toss him out through it. I had a smile on my face as I yelled, "OK." I could hear Father down there softly calling, "h-e-r-e kitty, kitty, kitty." Next thing we heard dad yell was "Gottcha!" Then father screamed at the top of his voice, "It's a SKUNK, hold open the door, here we come!"

Oh no, the wind must of blown the door shut and caused the lock to drop down. I tried to open it but first I needed to know for sure that it was really Father pounding on the door and not some maniac. Suddenly boards flew every where as Dad gave the door a giant kick. He looked like a wild man and smelled like one too! His eyes were blood red and watery. The skunk went left, I went right and so did Father. He was running after me and demanding me to stop, this just made me run faster.

We ran toward Aunt Leafy's place where they had four hound dogs in a pen. I was terrified that Father would catch me so I hit the latch on the dog pen. Soon they picked up the skunk scent that Father was wearing and tore out after him. Now Father was the hunted as I stopped and watched them disappear over a small hill. It was now the hounds could be heard baying, meaning something was treed.

Uncle Bob came running out with his shotgun asking me, if I had seen the critter the hounds were chasing. I told him I didn't see it but it smelled like a big skunk, as he raced off in the noisy direction. Well sir, Dad came home at sunset with a few scrapes and bruises and stinking to high heaven. He had to bury his skunk infested clothes and Mother ordered him to sleep in the barn. Next morning when we awoke rain was beating down in leaps and bounds. I heard Father open the kitchen and as he walked over to the table he didn't even yell at me, in fact he was so happy he gave me a hug along with a great big kick in the seat of my pants.

14

The Neahkanie Treasure

(In memory of Lloyd Grimes)

In 1967 Lloyd took a walk on the mountain. After a brief time of viewing the magnificent scenery of the Pacific Ocean he sat down on a boulder to have a cigarette. He dropped his flint lighter so he started searching around on the ground cover to find it. At the base of the boulder he was sitting on, he noticed some strange markings that were carved in the mossy granite.

He raced back to his car, grabbed his camera and snapped several pictures, which drew great attention, even that of a well-respected Tillamook attorney. The drawings on the rock showed two arrows, ten Spanish letters, a.w.t.w., and a series of dots.

The findings leaked out, so with sound advice the rock was removed and put under lock and key. Two pictures were sent to the university and after a careful study it was confirmed authentic and no doubt was carved in the late 1700s. I joined the excavation team along with twelve determined others. After a great deal of paper work we got out permits under the watchful eye of a state engineer who was paid to sit and watch our activities to assure no motor equipment would be used. The area was considered a state park.

Day one we picked and shoveled to the six-foot-level. Day two we dug down ten feet and day three—bingo, at the twelve-foot depth we hit rotten planks. After a study by a special agent the wood was determined to be oak. When we learned that oak wasn't native to the Neahkanie mountain our excitement exploded. The next day the digging continued but nothing important happened. Now the legend of the treasure states that the pirates, before buying the treasure, had chopped off the head of a slave then placed it on top of the treasure chest so the superstitious Indians wouldn't dig it back up. Next day we started getting discouraged, especially after getting a longer ladder as we reached the fifteen-foot level. We broke for lunch leaving the pit unattended. I had a plan but didn't think it would turn out to be such a terrible nightmare. Lloyd had an old wooden tool box sitting there by the pit with a bunch of rustic tools and pass-me-down junk inside. I also remembered some elk bones not far away, so with this knowledge I put my plan in motion.

I looked around and could see the diggers sitting in a circle enjoying their lunch, not paying any attention to me whatsoever. I lugged the tool box over to the pit and dropped it down the shaft, then shoveled dirt over the top of it. Next I gathered the bleached elk bones, dropped them down and also covered them with dirt. I hid behind some bushes and watched as the diggers moseyed towards the pit with shovels in hand.

It was Lloyd's turn to dig. I watched him disappear down the hole. The next sound I heard was "Yahoo, yahoo, we're rich, were rich!" Everyone gathered around and peered down the shaft shouting for joy. After discovering the bones he hit the old wooden tool box, that's when everyone went wild. Even the engineer broke his silence as he hurled his white hat high in the air and started jumping up and down. He told Lloyd not to open the chest until a major TV news crew got there along with a man from the historical society. We all ripped to the highway as the two-way radios were put in gear. People were stopping the traffic and yelling at the top of their voice that the Neahkanie treasure was found. Cars and people now were everywhere, running around the road, through the woods and all over the place.

I can't remember seeing so much excitement in one place. Later a new helicopter hovered above, then finally put down a cameraman and a lady newscaster who ran towards us, thinking they had the biggest story of the century. Microphones were humming as questions dominated the air. Police sirens screamed as an old man got hit by a car up on the highway, however, no attention was given him as more than fifty people flocked to the treasure pit. Seeing all this commotion I started to panic and harbored the thought of confessing my trick, but I didn't dare. I watched as Lloyd mounted the rickety old ladder and yelled for the rope. He made the up motion as the old box was cranked to the top. In all the excitement he didn't recognize his own tool box as it hit the ground. Cameras rolled as he popped the top. Now he looked stunned. His butt hit the ground as a microphone was shoved in his face. "How much do you think everything in that chest is worth?" asked the newsperson. Hearts sank when Lloyd said, "Oh, close to seven bucks." Folks pushed and shoved trying to peer into the box, but it was plain to see that the treasure had vanished, just like me.

The Miracle Man

The miracle man was coming to town and everyone was excited. He was from Halifax, the capital of Nova Scotia. Dad told us eight kids that his name was Abel, stating that he received this label because of his ability to perform miracles. Apparently at the age of fifty-five he was struck by lightning while fishing for herring in Peggy's Cove.

After leaving the hospital, ending his three-week stay, strange things began to happen. Father said he could make it rain during droughts, then stop the liquid flow anytime he wished.

I still remember cramming into Dad's Model-A, along with our entire family. The year was 1948, a beautiful August day, as we merrily bumped along the dirt road leading to the town's fairgrounds.

The place looked packed as Dad parked the hissing machine, excitement ran high as we marched inside the big arena. With a huge applause out came the miracle man. He was tall and slim with a brown derby hat and a handle bar mustache. He told the still crowd he would play the "Minute Waltz" on the piano blindfolded in sixty seconds without missing a note, a true miracle. You could hear a pin drop as he rolled up his sleeves and started pounding out the Minute Waltz. "He did it, he did it," the folks cried. However, the applause ended as the mayor jumped up and made the remark that Lib Chase, a native doughnut maker who was sitting next to him could play that same waltz just as blindfolded, and maybe even better. The miracle man bet twenty-five dollars she couldn't.

It took a lot of coaxing but Lib shyly made her way to the yellow-keyed piano. After being blindfolded she fired the music maker up. Her fingers seemed just like a blur as the old piano shook and rocked. The applause was tremendous, especially when the timekeeper announced, "She played the 'Minute Waltz' in fifty-six seconds." The applause and screams hurt my ears as Dad said he seen a little smoke arise from the hot keys.

Finally everyone settled down as Whit White, a sixty-year-old truck driver made his way up front on crutches. He was crippled one day when his truck, which he named the green hornet, left the road and ended upside down in a ditch.

The miracle man claimed he could make him walk again, but Whit's mother couldn't stand the action so she ran outside. After ten minutes she heard a thud, then a bunch of screams. Finally Uncle Bob ran out to her with the news as she anxiously listened. He began, "Well Bessie, the miracle man told him to throw away his left crutch, which he did, then he told him to throw away his right crutch, which he did." Bessie asked, "Yeah, yeah, what happened next?" Uncle Bob raised his raspy voice and replied, "What'd yaw think happened? He fell flat on his butt, he's crippled yaw know."

Well that was enough, everyone started yelling "fake, fake." Boy us kids were sure disappointed. We all piled back in the car making ready for home. Dad saw our sadness and suggested to Mother that we may as well stop at the soda shop for a treat. All agreed, so within minutes we were lapping at a double-decker ice cream cone. I told sister Ethel that I could finish my ice cream cone before her. Mother said that would be a miracle because Ethel was known to be the fastest ice cream eater on our road. I really think I could have won until I took a sharp pain over my right eye. Mother placed her warm hand on my head to ease the ache as she said, "This isn't a good day for miracles." Father also agreed as the ambulance screamed by with Whit White's bandaged legs sticking up in the back window.

Motorcycle Jump

Les Davis was a daredevil who lived up the road from us. He was thirty years old at the time and had a 1949 Harley Davidson motorcycle. I was seven years old and the year was 1952.

The whole town was in an uproar because Les was going to jump the Roseway River on his Harley. Halifax was the capital of Nova Scotia. They would send a news crew to report the event, and the city was even going to consume all expenses building the ramps, both take off and landing, plus make signs and sponsor the whole event.

Us kids was sure excited, especially when the trucks started arriving with lumber and other materials to build the tremendous jumping ramp. My dad was hired part-time to cut down trees, to clear brush all around the area as the big day was only three weeks away.

The town's band practiced every chance they got. Uncle Nic was the most important, he was to play the drum roll. Us kids would walk down there every day. It was exciting, especially when Les would go roaring by on his bike.

This one day we got more excitement than we bargained for. My aunt Hazel got knocked overboard when she tried to tell a professional ramp builder how to do his job. It was just like Mother said, "She was lucky there was a row boat nearby, because she didn't know how to swim."

The crew broke for lunch, cousin Harry and I hung around also, sometimes they would give us candy or gum. Everyone was sitting in the shade when Les tore by on his bike, however, this time a big shiny car was chasing him. We found out later it was the finance company. Father said he was at least six payments behind. This was terrible, only two days before the big jump, and no bike?

Somehow Les persuaded the banker to let him hold onto his machine until after the jump, then he would have enough money to pay all of his late payments. The morning of the jump a huge truck brought in seven bleachers for seating, another truck towed in a big trailer with cotton candy signs painted all over it. Us kids grew more excited by the minute, then at noon people started arriving by the dozens.

Les drove in with his bike on a trailer. It sure was beautiful, dark blue with red and white streamers dancing from his polished chrome handle bars. He kept walking up and down the ramp, checking every detail twice. The jump was fifty yards long across the river, with sharp rocks and fast water below.

One hour till jump time the band piped up with "Don't sit under the apple tree with anyone else but me." I bet in all there were six hundred people present, as the radio announcer burped his equipment on, then fire works lit up the blue sky. The mayor gave a speech as the Canadian Air Force flew over real low, to the surprise and delight of the huge crowd. I can't remember being so excited, as they received tremendous applause.

Now everyone's attention was focused on Les Davis when he kicked over the powerful Harley engine. No one was breathing. He got ready to make his historic leap. First he made a practice run partly up the ramp. Being satisfied with the workmanship he gave the thumbs up signal that he was ready.

I still remember seeing Les and the bike speeding up the ramp. His wife Thelma couldn't collect any life insurance because Les had neglected to take out any. However, the community grouped together and helped her out until she got back on her feet, 'cause Les never did.

The Bogeyman

When I was five years old the stories of the bogeyman frightened me very much. Our house was two stories and my bedroom was right at the top of the stairs, next to a big closet, where the bogeyman spent a lot of time as we were told. My mom hung a blanket where a door could have been, sealing off the closet and in my own reasoning, giving the bogeyman a delightful hiding spot.

This one night two of my friends decided to spend the night. Harry and Willy lived up the road. After supper we played outside until the sunlight faded like a melting ice cream cone. Soon we were off to bed and like always talk about the bogeyman hit high gear. Harry was seven years old and had as much wisdom as King Solomon or so I thought. Willy was six years old and scared of the dark, so he always packed a flash light to bed with him every night.

Harry made the remark that we should once and for all go in the closet and teach the bogeyman a lesson. Mother always told us if we didn't brush our teeth before going to bed the bogeyman might get us at midnight. We were sick and tired of "do this—do that, and if you don't, look out for the bogeyman." We started making plans that night by the dim light from Willy's flashlight. Harry would brainstorm the job, as he pointed to his head and said "little Einstein here." Both Willie and I agreed with a quick nod of our heads.

It was always said that the bogeyman came out at midnight. We heard the grandfather clock downstairs chime eleven, so we had one hour to make ready our attack. We had to shake Willie several times, trying to keep him awake, but it was no use, sleep overtook him. Harry said we didn't need him anyway, as he set our plan in motion. We quietly snuck towards the closet with Willie's flunky flashlight in hand. Harry's brilliant plan was to put two chairs on each side of the closet to stand on, then when the clocks struck twelve we would pull down the curtains over the never-seen bogeyman and kick and jump on him until he promised to leave our house and never return. I got to admit, I was plenty nervous and so was Einstein.

We stood up on the chairs, unhooked the woolly curtain and with heavy breathing, listened for the chiming of the clock downstairs. I could hear Hary's teeth clicking as the old curtain shook as if the wind was blowing. The time had finally come, but after the clock had chimed only seven times, my legs buckled as I fell head first into the dark closet, taking little Einstein with me. We busted a whole shelf full of strawberry preserves. Panic set in as Harry started crying so loud that it scared us even more. I tried to calm Harry down but he wanted out of there, just like me.

After running into the wall blindly several times we finally found our way out and back to our bedroom. We were still shaking, and now we could hear the bogeyman coming up the stairs. He was pushing on the door, we tried to hold it, but had to back off quickly. The bogeyman shot through, tripping over Harry while he was crawling under the bed. He was all white, very big and strong—I could tell this with the dim flashlight. I had to do something fast before he got up, so I grabbed Willy, who was still sleeping, and tossed him on the screaming bogeyman. Willy's backside landed in his face. I kicked the thing so hard I thought I had broken my toe. Boy were we surprised when the light went on. The bogeyman was Dad in his white long johns. Mother rushed in and smacked Father over the head with my toy tractor, then gave him a good scolding for scaring us kids.

A few days later Harry had another plan to capture the real bogeyman. However, I bailed out of his plans, having serious doubts about the wisdom of little Einstein, and somehow I sensed this was one subject we should not pursue any further.

15
They Got the Ax

Ene and Nelson were two twin brothers who lived down the road from us. They lived in a hen house converted into a humble home.

I was ten years old, the year was 1955 in a small Canadian town. Everyone used wood for heating and cooking, which in turn made cutting wood an important occupation. I don't remember them ever using power tools, just axes and bow saws, but my dad used to say they could chop more wood than a dozen hungry beavers.

Ene always told people that they went to school in Halifax and received a good education, but Father said the only time they went to school was to deliver a load of firewood and the only thing they received was a five dollar bill for their labor.

Ene was good with the ax, so he would chop wood and his brother Nelson would pile it. One day in October they were cutting wood for Brad Perry. It was a full five cords as Nelson piled it lopsided in Brad's woodshed. When they were making ready for home Ene went behind the high stack to relieve himself. A huge rumble brought Mr. Perry running from his house. Nelson was screaming like a bluejay being teased by a cat, he kept pointing and yelling that his brother was buried alive under five cords of wood that had fallen over on him. Brad and his wife Boo, along with Nelson, started frantically digging through the criss-cross fire wood hoping to find Ene alive and well. After almost an hour they uncovered the poor soul. He was grateful but was grieved because his chewing tobacco was missing. However, Brad awarded him with a brand-new plug.

One day they were cutting wood for the mayor when the ax flew off the handle and smashed through the windshield of the mayor's new car. Instead of facing the music they took off running after seeing that the mayor also flew off the handle. After dark they snuck back to retrieve their saw and coats along with two of the mayor's prized chickens, which no doubt filled their tummies for supper that evening. After two days in jail they made the announcement that a bus trip was in order, they were going to Halifax and apply for a wood cutting job with the government. That following Monday they boarded the Bullet, a tired bus that would take them to the remote Air Force base just outside of Halifax. The bus driver wasn't in a good mood, especially when he had to climb up on the bus roof to tie down their eight-foot crosscut saw, along with five wedges and two double-faced axes. What made him even madder is when they handed him up a wobbly old sawbuck. He hastily fastened them down with the other junk while giving them a new name. After a bunch of smoke and gear noise they were on their way. That evening some motorists who were ascending a steep hill, claimed they found a bunch of wood cutting tools which was identified to be the property of Ene and Nelson. It was five months later before anyone had heard from them again, then one Friday afternoon out plopped the twin brothers from the old smoking bus.

Father was driving home, so he offered them a ride to their place. They told Dad all about their journey and their experience with the government. Dad told it this way, as Nelson told it to him. "Ene and I got lost after getting off the bus. After three days of walking in the rain we finally found the air base. We were introduced to the chief of staff. He asked me first if I had a skill to give to the Air Force. I bluntly told him I was a pilot. He was excited and yelled to his aide to make arrangements to join me up. As the aide walked me to the headquarters I thought it was strange that there wasn't any wood piles around. The general then asked my brother Ene what skills he had, he told him he was a wood chopper. The general laughed and told him they didn't need any wood choppers. Ene got mad and asked, why then did you hire my brother? The general gruffly said, 'cause he's a pilot." Ene then said, "That ain't fair, I have to chop the wood before he can pile it!"

P.S.—Nelson and Ene later in years owned three saw mills, retired wealthy men, then married twin sisters. In 1992 the government nailed them for tax evasion, giving them the ax!

The Counterfeiter

It was one of those days on the farm that made us kids feel special. Warm sunny blue skies. The big oak trees started showing off their size by casting giant shadows. I was seven years old this day back in 1952, when Norm Enzer tore up the road, driving his old Studebaker of three colors, raising a trail of dust as he whipped into our driveway.

He was a robust turkey farmer who owned a farm twelve miles up the road, but today for some reason started tooting his horn with something on his mind. Us seven kids raced to his jalopy as steam sprayed from the tired radiator sounding like geese going south. Mother stepped out from the kitchen smelling like fresh baked bread as she wiped her hands on the stained worn apron that had seen two generations. Norm yanked the newspaper from his back seat. It read, "Counterfeiter believed to be in the county." This was terrific news, our town needed some excitement. The news spread fast, everyone was pointing fingers and a lot of unfair words were spoken, causing trouble among friends.

I didn't know what a counterfeiter was so I jumped on my bicycle and rode to Harry's place. He had tons of wisdom, even though he was only eight. His mother said he had the mind of a nine year old.

The newspaper said that six Mounties from Halifax were coming to town, and would pay a twenty-five-dollar reward for information leading to an arrest. I talked to Harry and we discussed what we would do with the money, all right! New bicycles for both of us! I was so proud of Harry, he was using his powerful mind when he said, "I know who the counterfeiter is." I yelled yahoo-yahoo with glee, and for a moment could even smell the fresh red paint on the new Flyers.

Down the road came my Aunt Hazel on her bicycle, she was peddling so fast it looked as if her feet were turning backwards. I told Harry there was no way she could make the sharp turn into our driveway. Her polka-dot dress trailed up behind her like a blanket on a clothes line during a wind storm. Then it happened. She started sliding in the dirt, sounded like someone blowing their nose that had a bad cold. I bet she rolled a dozen times as Harry and I ran to help her up, but she started yelling at us, blaming us for her scraped knees and missing wig. We finally got her to the house as Mom gave her Watkins salve, which boasted on the label, good for man or beast.

Harry and I headed for town to report the counterfeiter. We spit on our hands to brush our hair in place, then walked into the office where sat a gruff old sergeant Mountie. Harry told him the counterfeiter was Uncle Lew. He got up, grabbed us by our shirts, pulled us up to his weathered face and yelled out questions. I remember his hot breath smelled like fresh cow manure. Moments later he signaled the five other Mounties to mount up. Boy this was exciting, they even strapped on pistols with real bullets. They ordered Harry and me to lead the way on our bikes. Somehow the news got out, 'cause behind the horses were two dozen folks.

When we arrived at Uncle Lew's place, Harry pointed to a large shop in the backyard. He explained that one day he dropped in and watched Uncle Lew counter fitting. The Mounties drew their guns, rushed the shop, kicking down the floor. From where we stood the sound of lumber could be heard hitting the floor along with Uncle Lew. He sure looked surprised when they marched him outside, his eyes were big and his hair was standing straight up. The Mounties wrecked the shop, turning over tables and pulling one wall apart looking for evidence. Finding none they ordered Harry and me inside to show them where the illegal items were. Harry pointed to a freshly made cupboard, then to three newly fitted counters. It was now that they discovered that Uncle Lew was a cabinet maker. I couldn't help but thinking that Harry wasn't very smart.

The gruff sergeant again grabbed us, pulled us up to his face and started yelling as he said, "I can tell you boys have learned your lesson cause I can see tears in your eyes." I nervously spoke up and said, "Sir, the tears are because your breath smells like fresh cow manure." Now he really got mad, told us to get home, which we did and so did everyone else, except Uncle Lew, he went to his shop, and again started counter fitting.

Here's to Ya

Uncle Lou had a farm and on that farm he had many animals, but the one he favored most was a pig he named Nipper. Us kids would visit the farm and Nipper, being very curious, would always greet us with a squeal and a wagging tail. Uncle Lou was a laid back farmer and always seemed to have a lot of cash. It's just like Aunt Hazel said, "He must be doing something crooked, he should be run clear out of town before he is proven innocent."

It seems everyone loved Uncle Lou and his pig, except Aunt Hazel. She would smack the poor thing with a broom when it wandered over towards her land. In late spring everyone would plant their garden. Small cucumbers were the main product because competition at the county fair for the best homemade pickles was a fierce contest.

Aunt Hazel had won every year but this year Uncle Lou announced that he would enter the main event with his special recipe. Poor Aunt Hazel, she worked well into late evening nurturing her pickle crop, then scattering what she called top secret ingredients all around them to insure a first trophy win at the fair.

One day when she heard that Uncle Lou was also entering the event, and that he too had a secret ingredient, she told big mouth Elma Short, the town crier, that Lou's ingredients was raw material that he shoveled out of 'old smokey', our outhouse.

After reading this statement from the newspaper Uncle Lou raced over to Aunt Hazel's place and called her a busybody and a big mouth, then he stuck out his tongue at her. Aunt Hazel grabbed it and swung him around until his feet left the ground. It's just like Mother said, "He's lucky his tongue was slippery, causing Aunt Hazel to loose her grip. She could have pulled it clean out." Poor Uncle Lou couldn't

156

talk or eat for three days, but his first words were, "What made her do that?"

Uncle Lou wouldn't let good enough alone. When he seen Aunt Hazel pass by on her bike heading for town, he turned Nipper, his pig, loose in her garden. In no time at all not a pickle could be seen, as the pig burped all the way back to Lou's farm with a belly full of cucumbers. Uncle Lou climbed a tall oak tree overlooking Hazel's garden, well hidden from view, or so he thought. He watched as Aunt Hazel wheeled her bike in the yard. She spotted what once was her garden, then her temper flared after spotting pig tracks. Her wild actions scared Lou so bad he began to shake, as acorns rattled loose from the tree limb where he was perched. Aunt Hazel gazed upward as Uncle Lou started crying. Later he told a friend her face looked that of a wolverine and he stated how terrified he was as giant muscles in her back rippled while bending over to pick up a rock. His screams along with her yelling brought my dad along with my uncles to Uncle Lou's rescue.

The next day two men in suits arrived from Halifax, explained to Dad that they needed to inspect the outhouse because of a complaint concerning outlawed fertilizer for crop use. As they approached old smokey they suddenly stopped, then asked father, "Is there a bear in there growling?" Father said, "No, that's Grampa, he is colorblind, put prune juice on his corn flakes this morning instead of milk." Both well-dressed men held their noses, which made their voices change when they said "Phew". Uncle Lou got a chewing out but wasn't charged with unlawful use of prohibited fertilizer.

The day finally arrived for the fair. Us kids sure was excited as we piled into the car. Uncle Lou stopped us when we pulled out of the driveway, held up a jar of his pickles while making the remark that he should win especially now that Aunt Hazel couldn't enter the contest. We noticed Nipper, his pig, wasn't with him like always, so we asked about him. Uncle Lou said he must have run off. He couldn't find him anywheres, but was sure he'd return as usual.

The fair was exciting, then came the contests. Sure enough, Uncle Lou took first place for his pickles. We congratulated him as he patted me on the back and said, "You and your family had a lot to do with it." At that time I didn't know what he meant. All of a sudden he spotted Aunt Hazel, raised his first place trophy up and laughed. Aunt Hazel also raised her first place trophy up and also laughed, just as the judge said, "This is the best doggone bacon I've ever tasted."

Teaching Rusty a Lesson

We gathered outside of the old schoolhouse discussing what we should do about Rusty. He was bigger and older than the rest of us kids in grade four. This one day he put a thumbtack on the teacher's chair. This cost us two recesses on a beautiful April day.

He would bend all the rules when we played any kind of a game. At the ball games he would swing at the ball until he hit it no matter how many strikes he had. He always gave our teacher Mrs. Smith a bad time everyday, until she would cry. He would corner poor Willy and slap him silly until he gave up his milk money. I had a sweetheart and she was eight and her name was Jenny. Rusty, this one day pushed her down, skinning her knees up pretty good. When I heard this I told the other kids, enough is enough, we got to teach Rusty a good lesson.

Saturday morning we gathered down by the lake and held a meeting in Rusty's honor. Now down the road there was an old house that sat back in the woods, not visible from the road. Ever since us kids could walk and talk we were told that an old hermit had once lived there and had beheaded at least six kids with his ax. We will kept clear of the place because of this and as the story goes his ghost was still active in the cellar.

Rusty would laugh and call us cowards each time we would talk about the old Crawford house, so this gave us an idea. Friday morning six of us kids were walking to school and just like always Rusty could be seen learning on the old oak tree waiting for Willy with his milk money. Willy wasn't with us this time so we explained to Rusty that Willy went to the old Crawford house and had not returned. We told Rusty we would give him our milk money if he would go and rescue him. He agreed but demanded our milk money for a whole month and if we didn't cough it up he would leave us all toothless.

Now our teacher's husband was in on our plan and he could impersonate and was well known for his transparent abilities. He had a good plan. All we had to do was make sure Rusty made it inside the haunted house. The stage was set, so when the bell rang Mrs. Smith winked letting us know that her husband would be dressed in his skeleton suit to greet Rusty inside the haunted house. Twelve of us kids followed Rusty but ducked behind the bushes about twenty-five yards from the house.

Willy showed up shaking with excitement and kept talking about how he would get to taste milk at lunch time again. We watched Rusty pull open the mossy groaning back door and enter the old house. Someone tipped him off. A dreadful scream exited the cellar door, out shot Mr. Smith in his skeleton suit being chased by the hunchbacked scar faced old man wielding his axe. Later we learned it was Rusty wearing a mask dressed in raggedy old black pants.

Mr. Smith screamed so loud that he split his Adam's apple and Mother said even today he could call in all kinds of birds, even the rare bald eagle. Poor Ethel was so terrified that when she was old enough to date, her boy friends would always make remarks about her big eyes. Mother would laugh and say the old Crawford house incident had something to do with that. Ethel would leave the room crying. Willy panicked, causing him to leave a trail resembling a salted slug. Poor Ray, even to this day he will only work day shift jobs. I was so terrified that I had burn marks on my legs from running. Mother said this was caused from friction of the snapping of my pant legs. As for Harry, even to this day he suffers from shock. His mother wrote and said he will often wear a bed pan on his head claiming to be a British soldier.

Oh well, we didn't fix Rusty, he won again, but when we heard he and his family was moving to New Brunswick we threw a party. But you know, maybe we had won after all. We kept wanting to give Rusty the ax—and that day at the Crawford house he actually had one.